FROM TAX POPULISM TO ETHNIC NATIONALISM

Radical Right-Wing Populism in Sweden

Jens Rydgren

Berghahn Books
New York • Oxford

First published in 2006 by

Berghahn Books
www.berghahnbooks.com

©2006 Jens Rydgren

Library of Congress Cataloging-in-Publication Data
Rydgren, Jens.
  [Från skattemissnöje till etnisk nationalism. English]
  From tax populism to ethnic nationalism : radical right-wing populism in
Sweden / Jens Rydgren.
    p. cm.
  Includes bibliographical references and index.
  ISBN 1-84545-218-6 (hardback : alk. paper)
    1. Political parties—Sweden.   2. Populism—Sweden.   3. Right-wing
extremists—Sweden.   4. Sweden—Politics and government—1973–
  I. Title.

JN7995.A1R93 2006
324.2485'03—dc22   2006013686

British Library Cataloguing in Publication Data
A catalogue record for this book is available from the British Library

Printed in the United States on acid-free paper

ISBN 1-84545-218-6 hardback

To my wife, Malin Wahlberg

CONTENTS

ILLUSTRATIONS

Figures

Tables

ACKNOWLEDGMENTS

Foremost I want to thank my colleagues at the Department of Sociology at Stockholm University, at which most of this book has been written. Sidney Tarrow had the kindness to host me at the Department of Government at Cornell University during some productive weeks during the fall of 2004, for which I am very grateful. I also owe thanks to the Swedish Cooperation in Research and Higher Education (STINT), who generously funded my visit to Cornell.

I am also much indebted to Göran Ahrne, Elisabeth Elgán, and Anders Widfeldt, who have read and commented on drafts of this book.

Chapter 2 is based on my article "Is Extreme Right-wing Populism Contagious? Explaining the Emergence of a New Party Family," *European Journal of Political Research* 2005, 44: 1–25. Chapter 5 partly builds on my article "Radical Right Populism in Sweden: Still a Failure, But for How Long?," *Scandinavian Political Studies* 2002, 25 (1): 27–56.

This study has been financially supported by two grants from the Swedish Research Council, (2002–3371) and (422–2004–255).

INTRODUCTION

In their seminal article written in the mid 1960s, Lipset and Rokkan (1967) argued that Western European party systems had become "frozen." New political parties were able to establish themselves only with immense difficulty, and already extant ones very much reflected the axes of conflict that had crystallized in the 1920s or earlier. Of these, the economic class dimension, which pits labor against capital, dominated the twentieth century, although also even older conflict dimensions, such as the conflicts between church and state or between center and periphery, still were—and are—salient in many countries.

However, much has happened in the more than thirty years since Lipset and Rokkan's article: the party systems in Western Europe have grown more destabilized and two new political families have emerged. The mid 1970s saw environmental parties gain ground in several countries, and in Sweden the Green Party won seats in the parliament, the Riksdag, in 1988. Earlier in the 1970s, populist protest parties also started to emerge in Denmark and Norway. The Danish Progress Party, led by Mogens Glistrup, was founded in 1972 and reaped 15.9 percent of the votes in the 1973 election. Glistrup's success inspired Anders Lange to form a similar party in Norway, which later in 1973 won 5 percent of the vote. Contrary to expectations, these parties did not evaporate as quickly as they had appeared; in Denmark the Progress Party started to wane only with the formation of *Dansk Folkeparti* (the Danish People's Party)—another right-wing populist party—while in Norway electoral support for the Progress Party has strengthened since the end of the 1980s (Goul Andersen & Bjørklund 2000; Bjørklund & Goul Andersen 2002; Rydgren 2004a).

Nevertheless, these types of populist party, which primarily mobilized against bureaucracy and a tax pressure that in their opinion had escalated out of all proportion, failed to spread to the other Western European countries. No similar party managed to achieve success on a national scale in Sweden, either, during the 1970s and 1980s, even if a number of local and regional parties—headed by the southern regional *Skånepartiet* (the Skåne Party)—won mandates in municipal councils with a message heavily inspired by Denmark's Progress Party (see Peterson et al. 1989).

Instead, a new party family evolved in the 1980s and 1990s. These parties, which I will refer to in this book as Radical Right-Wing Populist (RRP) parties, have the characteristic trait of *sharing the fundamental ideological core of ethnonationalist xenophobia (based on the "ethnopluralistic" doctrine) and antiestablishment populism* (see Rydgren 2005). Unless newly founded, these parties have their roots either in extraparliamentary right-wing extremism or in populist protest movements or parties. Today, this new party family would include the French Front National, the Austrian FPÖ, and the Danish People's Party, among several others (see Betz & Immerfall 1998; Ignazi 2003; Hainsworth 2000; Schain et al. 2002; Rydgren & Widfeldt 2004). Sverigedemokraterna (the Sweden Democrats), which is today's leading RRP party in Sweden, traces its lineage back to Swedish extraparliamentary right-wing extremism, and since the end of the 1990s has gradually become a more full-fledged RRP party combining ethnonationalism and xenophobia with a right-wing authoritarian take on sociocultural issues and a populist political message. However, compared to most other RRP parties in Western Europe, the Sweden Democrats are marginalized in terms of electoral support.

The fact is that Sweden can be considered something of an anomaly when it comes to right-wing populism, which has been a relative failure in a Western European perspective. Apart from the 1991 election, when the newly formed *Ny Demokrati* (New Democracy) garnered 6.7 percent of the vote, and the brief period between 1991 and 1993 when it received good results in the opinion polls, Swedish right-wing populist parties have never managed to attract more than at most 1.5 percent of the electorate. New Democracy is interesting per se, as it cannot be fitted into either of the above categories. Even if we find in New Democracy influences from the tax-populist Danish and Norwegian Progress Parties, much of its populist opposition to tax and the state were also rooted in *New Welfare*, the think tank funded by the Swedish Employers' Confederation (SAF). At the same time, as we will discover in the following chapters, there were also distinct traces of the anti-immigration and xenophobic rhetoric typical of the RRP parties. However, ethnonationalism, and especially "ethnopluralism," were not particularly strong features of New Democracy's political message, and so I am more inclined to see it as a hybrid of taxpopulism and radical right-wing populism and am reluctant to include it among the RRP party family.

The aim of this book is to trace the development of right-wing populism in Sweden, both tax populism and radical right-wing populism, over the past fifteen years. Rather than simply confining myself to describing its chronology (although this will of course be dealt with), I will try to explain the conditions behind its rise and popular success—or failure. As mentioned above, in Sweden it is very much a case of the latter.

This book will be structured in a straightforward way: First, radical right-wing populism will be defined. Secondly, I will outline a theoretically based model for explaining the emergence of electoral successful (radical) right-wing populist parties in some Western European countries, and the lack thereof in other countries. The remaining chapters will use this explanatory model in explaining the emergence of the party New Democracy in the 1991 election (in chapter 3), why this party broke apart and disappeared only a few years later (in chapter 4), and why no other Swedish (radical) right-wing populism has emerged on the national political arena since 1994 (in chapter 5).[1]

Notes

1. A short methodological note: In order to deal with the aims of this study, a certain degree of methodological pluralism has been needed. When discussing the so-called demand-side of politics, the secondary literature has been a great help. I have also used primary data, in particular data from the "Swedish Election Survey" 1991 (SSD 0391) primarily collected by Michael Gilljam and Sören Holmberg at Gothenburg University, and conducted a series of logistic regression analyses in order to explain the vote for New Democracy in 1991. Ideally, I would have included similar analyses, testing the same models, for explaining the vote for New Democracy in the 1994 election and the vote for the Sweden Democrats in the 2002 election. However, there were too few voters in the samples having voted for these parties, which made the estimations too unreliable. As a result, they have not been included. For the so-called supply-side of politics, I have used quotes from party programs and the internal party press of New Democracy and the Sweden Democrats in order to show the way these parties have tried to take advantage of existing political opportunities for electoral mobilization. I have also used a large number of newspaper reports, and when appropriate the secondary literature.

1

What Are Tax Populism and Radical Right-Wing Populism?

Populism is an often-abused term, and is often used as a way of stigmatizing political opponents or as a label with which to brand politicians or parties harboring aspirations to be "popular." Consequently, the concept has been bled of meaning, and should therefore be carefully defined before being used as a descriptive or analytical tool. In this chapter I will be making a distinction between populist *ideology* and populist *strategy*. The parties and political currents under discussion in the coming pages have in common their adoption of a populist strategy and their shared allegiance, to differing degrees, to a common populist ideology.

Populist ideology

The defining features of populist ideology are an aversion or even a hostility toward the concept of representative democracy (which in a democratic context is often manifested as a demand for more direct democracy); a notion of "the people" as a harmonic and homogenous collective—and of the "elite" or the "establishment" as essentially different from "the people"; and the belief that the party or leader represents the voice of "the people." I will be expanding on these points below, but before we continue I would like to stress that populist ideology is rarely found in its pure form when we examine actual political parties or movements. This is, of course, also true for other political ideologies, but it is particularly salient in the case of populism (see Taggart 2000: 3f). These movements combine the populist ideology (and few populist parties embrace *all* the items discussed below) with other standpoints and values, and historically speaking such movements have taken up a position on both the political left and right—even though what we normally find is that populists claim allegiance to neither (Canovan 1984: 294; Rydgren 2003b: chap. 6; Worsley 1969: 241).

The populist view of democracy

Unlike neofascism and other forms of extraparliamentary right-wing extremism, populism does not define itself outside democracy. Populist movements also seek political legitimacy by professing to represent the voice of the people, and prefer to see themselves as a medium for the "will of the people" (Berlin et al. 1968: 173ff). Despite this, populism generally harbors a mistrust of government institutions and other mainstream public bodies, such as political parties, government administration, universities, and the media, something that is largely attributed to the more general antipathy toward elites and elite values (Canovan 1999: 3). In the eyes of populist parties and movements, elites, particularly of the political kind, are corrupt and devoid of the "common sense" with which the common man is blessed (Shils 1956: 101ff). This also applies, perhaps even particularly so, to the democratic, representative institutions, which are seen as being distanced from "the people." Apart from corruption, which is considered the main reason for politicians "not caring about what people think," there are also what populists would refer to as "special interests," which divert political attention from the public interest when political decisions are being made. Just what these special interests are tends to vary from one populist movement or party to another. Right-wing populists point to immigrants and other ethnic minorities, feminists and gay societies and so on, while left-wing populists stress big money, multinational corporations, and private bankers (Taggart 2000: 93).

As a result of their antipathy toward political elites, which they accuse of dominating representative democracy, populists advocate direct democracy (see Ménu & Surel 2000: 61). Given that the term "democracy" is, at least in everyday usage, both nebulous and ambiguous and open to different interpretations, populists are able to achieve a certain measure of credibility in their claim that representative democracy is an obstacle to what they consider the "true" democracy: direct democracy (see Rydgren 2003b: chap. 6).

The populist notion of "the people"

As we can see, "the people" occupy a key position in the populist ideology. However, it is not always clear what—or rather, whom—the concept comprises. In order to be able to present "the people" as a monolithic group, which is to say as a homogeneous collective free of internal conflict and variation, populist movements exclude, explicitly or implicitly, certain groups from their definition of the term. The identity of such excluded groups depends to a certain extent on the movement in question, even though they all consider the "elite" or the "establishment" as divorced from the people. Most populist parties and movements also equate the conceptual confines of "the people" with those of the nation; some of them, such as the RRP parties, also adopt an ethnonationalist view of the people that encompasses exclusively those who belong to their own ethnic nationality. Consequently immigrants and other ethnic minorities are excluded, as very often are international and cosmopolitan actors and organizations (see Rydgren 2003b: chap. 6; Ménu & Surel 2000: 217f; Stewart 1969; Taggart 2000: 92; Canovan 1999: 5).

Paul Taggart uses the term "heartland" to visualize how populists construe the term "the people." What Taggart (2000: 3, 95) maintains is that populist ideology is often built upon an explicit or implicit idealized picture of a chosen people living in an equally idealized geographical area, or heartland. For certain populist movements, this idealized area coincides with that contained within the nation's borders; for others, it is the regional borders that matter. Both heartland types are drawn by looking both inwards and backwards in that the idea they embody is based on the supposed homogeneous, genuine lifestyle that characterized an idealized past; that is to say, on the concept of a spontaneous and naturally governed *gemeinschaft* (see also MacRae 1969: 155f).

Another consequence of the monolithic idea of "the people" is the denial of class differences and conflicts. Class interests are seen as special interests, and populist parties and movements often present themselves as the "classless" champions of the *people*, unlike other parties that are said to promote special interests to the exclusion of all others. Populists therefore use the terms "the common people" or "the man in the street" rather than "the working class" when appealing to potential voter groups (Rydgren 2003b: chap. 6; Worsley 1969: 241). As mentioned above, populists believe that "common sense" is the reserve of "the people" and not the elite, who are instead encumbered by bureaucratic absurdity and theoretical knowledge of no practical value.

A populist political economy

The populist ideology opposes centralization, the division of labor, class thinking, mass production, the globalization of the economy, and "economistic" reasoning (i.e., that economic growth is the one and only goal) (see Fryklund & Peterson 1981; Mény & Surel 2000: 217f). For populists, all these features of society threaten the *gemeinschaft* for which they yearn, and thus alienate the people from their former integrated lives. They are also associated with the "elite," who by definition act contrary to the interests of the people, and with the political ideologies (be they liberal or socialist) populists despise. The alternative advocated by populism is an economic policy based on small-scale production and family capitalism (Fryklund & Peterson 1981; Mény & Surel 2000). Even though populist parties and movements at times might oppose economic inequality, it is usually economic inequality caused by institutions they dislike. Otherwise, they generally do not favor principally egalitarian economic policies.

Anti-intellectualism

Populists often advocate policies based on political simplifications, even if few of them would put it like that themselves. Ideally, politics should be direct, to the point, and rooted firmly in common sense, while political solutions should be worded in a way that "common people" can understand (Taggart 2000: 97, 112). Many populists also argue that most political issues *are* far simpler than the mainstream parties would have us believe. To them, the "political class," a term populists like to use, deliberately portrays political issues as abstruse and complex in its endeavors to keep "the people" alienated, and to thereby appropriate all power for itself (Canovan 1981: 208).

Following this reasoning, populist parties and movements prefer more transparent decision-making processes, such as referenda. They are almost by principle skeptical of all nontransparent aspects of day-to-day *realpolitik*, such as political compromises, (secret) deals, and the technical jargon typical of reports and committees (see Canovan 1999: 6).

Populist strategy: the antiestablishment strategy

The populist antiestablishment strategy, as illustrated in Figure 1, is based on populist parties' endeavor to create an image of being in opposition to the entire political establishment while not for that reason antidemocratic or even too politically extreme (Schedler 1996).

An effective way for a populist party to distance itself from the mainstream political parties (i.e., the government party or parties and the "normal" opposition parties) is to deny the plurality of political persuasions that the different parties represent by claiming that in reality they

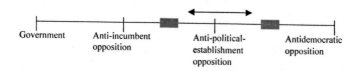

Figure 1.1. The populist antiestablishment strategy
Source: Schedler (1996: 303).

constitute one single, relatively homogeneous political class. Populists often maintain, for instance, that the differences between the government and the established opposition are just irrelevant superficialities, and that the rivalry shown by these parties is nothing more than a sham. The political class is often accused of having misappropriated power from the people, something that convinces the populists that a new party is needed to defend the interests and wishes of the common man. They thus promote their own party as the only real alternative to the establishment: no other genuine opposition exists.

At the same time, the populist party must be careful not to appear antidemocratic or too politically extreme. Since an overwhelming majority of the electorate in all Western European countries supports democracy and sees antidemocratic organizations as highly illegitimate, being branded an antidemocratic extremist party would be a stigma that would severely hinder their vote-winning potential. This aspect of the populist antiestablishment strategy is particularly important for the RRP parties that have emerged from the extraparliamentary far right (such as the Sweden Democrats). These parties can find it exceedingly hard work to wash away their antidemocratic label, and until they can erect a more respectable façade, they will find it very difficult to evade electoral marginalization.

Tax populism and radical right-wing populism

It is obviously an empirical question how well these points fit the different right-wing populist parties that we will be discussing in this book. As I mentioned above, all of them adopt the populist antiestablishment strategy; however, since other new Swedish parties (e.g., the Green Party) have also done so, it can hardly be considered a sufficient condition for defining a party as populist rather than anything else (even if the Green Party, at least during its early years, could partly be classified as populist for other reasons too). As we will see, there are also elements of populist ideology in the parties we will be discussing, albeit of varying importance and significance. The tax populist Scandinavian progress parties can be said to have occupied a position close to the populist ideological ideal as outlined above, especially during the 1970s (see Fryklund & Peterson 1981), and the same can be said of regional right-wing populist parties, such as the Skåne Party, during the 1980s (Peterson et al. 1989). New Democracy, on the other hand, had neoliberalism as one of its central ideological pillars, and as we will discover in later chapters, the party deviated in a number of ways from the populist ideal.

The rest of this chapter, however, will be devoted to contemporary RRP parties (including the Sweden Democrats), a political family that is as close to the nationalistic far right as it is to populism. As shown above, the RRP parties are recognized by the way in which their political manifestos and profiles are based on a blend of ethnonationalist xenophobia (based on the "ethnopluralistic" doctrine) and the populist antiestablishment strategy. This latter has already been discussed, and I will give a brief account of the former before proceeding.

The ethnonationalist, ethnopluralist doctrine first took shape within the French *Nouvelle Droite* (New Right) in the 1970s. This doctrine, which forms the basis of what is referred to as "neo-racism" (Barker 1981) or "cultural racism" (Wieviorka 1998: 32), was launched as an alternative to the old sociobiological concept of race. Taking the French leftwing idea of *difference*—which forms the basis of the multicultural doctrine (i.e., that immigrants must be entitled to retain the customs and traditions of their countries of origin should they so wish)—the ethnopluralist doctrine maintains that different nationalities or ethnicities must be kept separate lest their unique cultural characteristics disappear and they cease to be distinct folk groups or ethnicities (Minkenberg 1997; Taguieff 1988). In this way, the New Right in France saw French culture and traditions as being under threat from immigrant Muslims from North Africa. A further theme of this doctrine is that different cultures and ethnicities are incompatible, and can never join in peaceful coexistence. A peaceful society, according to the ethnopluralists, requires an ethnically homogeneous population. Even though this doctrine is clearly based on a deterministic and monolithic view of culture and ethnicity (ignoring the potential for personal change and variation within the various ethnicities), unlike traditional racism it is not necessarily hierarchical. Different nationalities or ethnicities are not automatically seen as being of a higher or lower status, but simply as different and incompatible. Armed with the ethnopluralist doctrine, RRPs have been able to use a xenophobic message without becoming as stigmatized as the "old-school" racists had been during the postwar years (see Rydgren 2005).

It should also be mentioned that the RRP parties are "right-wing" mainly when it comes to sociocultural issues. In addition to their (particularly restrictive) views on immigration and citizenship, the RRP parties often have a staunchly conservative or even authoritarian outlook on issues such as law and order (tougher punishment) and the family (advocating traditional gender roles and renouncing feminism). Things become more blurred, however, on economic issues. Although over time large changes can be detected as well as considerable variations within the RRP party family, a general trend is discernible. While in the 1980s most RRP parties shared a form of neoliberalism toward the public economy, since the 1990s most of them have drifted toward a middle-ground position that defends the welfare state. "Welfare chauvinism" has become an increasingly potent rhetorical weapon for these parties, who blame the problems encumbering the welfare state (e.g., low pensions and long hospital queues) on the cost of immigration. We ought to stress, however, that economic issues have never been the main concern for the RRP parties, which is why it has always been relatively easy for them to shift their footing on such matters. Instead, these parties are essentially *culturalistic*, and they lay the stress on *values* rather than *material* things.

The main reason why I have chosen to label these parties extremist is that they embody a spirit of *antipluralism*, or monism. As Lipset and Raab (1970: 6) have asserted, the "operational heart of extremism is the repression of difference and dissent, the closing down of the market place of ideas. More precisely, the operational essence of extremism, or monism, is the tendency to treat cleavage and ambivalence as *illegitimate*." Political monism or antipluralism have traditionally manifested themselves in the ranks of the far right in two different ways: as opposition toward, and/or a denial of, the democratic political *system*; and as opposition toward and/or denial of universal and egalitarian *values* (or "democratic" values), such as the Human Rights Convention, or more specifically the concept of equality in the eyes of the law (see Rydgren 2003b). As we have seen above, the RRP parties do not claim to be opponents of democracy as a political system, despite their critical or openly hostile attitude toward representative democracy. On this point they are populist. Yet they also have a monistic value base, opposing and/or denying pluralistic values. As historian Zeev Sternhell (1986: 2) has argued, and partly demonstrated, "ideology that propounds an organic society is bound to be unsympathetic to political pluralism." Even though the term "ethnopluralism" suggests otherwise, the xenophobic ethnonationalism espoused by the RRP parties is an example of such an organic ideology. Their value-based, culturalistic ideology is based even more generally on the notion of "the natural order" (see Rydgren 2003b). While everything that is considered consistent with this harmonic and organic natural order (as manifested, for example, in the nation and the family) is considered desirable and "good," everything that disrupts this order (immigration, ethnic mixing, feminism, and homosexuality) is condemned.

2

WHY DO RIGHT-WING POPULIST PARTIES ARISE?

In later chapters we will be discussing the rise of the party New Democracy in the early 1990s, and the reasons for the lack of popularly successful RRP parties in Sweden since 1994. In doing so we will be using a theoretical model that has proved useful for understanding the rise of the Front National in France (Rydgren 2003b) and the Danish People's Party (Rydgren 2004a). This model requires us to examine (1) the presence or absence of favorable political opportunity structures and (2) how successfully emerging or embryonic parties have managed to take advantage of existing niches and other favorable opportunity structures. This latter compels us to also examine (3) the political profiles and strategies of the emergent parties and (4) their organizational structures and access to essential resources. These four phases of the model will be discussed in turn below.

Political opportunity structures

Sidney Tarrow (1998: 19f) has defined political opportunity structures as "consistent—but not necessarily formal, permanent or national" resources that are external in relation to the parties or social movements under study. Even if the term opportunity *structure* might suggest the contrary, some of the mechanisms to be discussed under this heading are more situational than stable and lasting (see Tarrow 1998). There is, however, reason to believe that stable, relatively permanent political opportunity structures *and* those that are more unstable together help us understand why new parties—in this case right-wing populist parties—are able to emerge. We might suppose the former group to be of particular relevance to explaining differences *between* countries (i.e., why such parties have struck a popular chord in certain countries but failed in others), while it sheds less light on why there are variations over time *within* countries (or political systems). The latter group we can take to be the converse (see Rydgren 2005).

If, then, a new party—in this case a right-wing populist party—is to emerge and win the support of a significant proportion of the electorate, some (but not all) of the following political opportunity structures must be present:

(1) Let us begin with the most general opportunity structure: the appearance of niches in the electoral arena (see Rydgren 2003b). This is a composite notion comprising many of the mechanisms discussed below, particularly under "Dealignment/Realignment" and "The politicization of new political issues."

We may assume that no new parties will emerge if (A) there are no sufficiently large niches, which can be defined as the gap between the position of the voters and the perceived position of the parties in the same political space (i.e., as a given demand not being satisfied by a corresponding supply); and (B) there is a high proportion of voters with a high degree of party identification. Niches sometimes appear as a result of the time lag between the movements of the voters and the parties in political space. When public opinion changes course, the political parties have to adapt their profiles accordingly, lest they lose voters (Downs 1957; Rydgren 2003b); political parties, however, are not as flexible and quick to change as voter opinion and so these time lags develop. Despite this, niches of any significant size rarely appear under normal, relatively stable circumstances as the parties have had a fair amount of time to locate their optimal positions. Instead, they normally open up only in the event of rapid and dramatic shifts in public opinion or when one or more of the larger mainstream parties make radical changes to their political profile. If a new party is able to maintain a political profile that matches the vacant niche, it will have a good chance of attracting voter support, especially if the proportion of voters with strong party identity is relatively low (see Rydgren 2003b: chap. 1).

The chances of a niche appearing are higher if a new or previously weak cleavage dimension, or a political issue associated with such a dimension, suddenly becomes increasingly salient (at the expense of the dominant cleavage dimension). When this happens, the mainstream parties have not had the incentive or the opportunity to position themselves strategically within the alternative cleavage dimension, and are often gathered together in relatively dense clusters, which opens up one or more niches big enough for the new parties to exploit.

Many Western European countries have also seen their voter arenas become more volatile over the past decades, something which has often been combined with relatively dramatic changes in the attitudes and preferences of the electorate (Kitschelt 1995; Rydgren 2003b). One of the causes of this is profound macro-transformations, such as the transition from an industrial to a postindustrial economy and the related process of economic and cultural globalization. There have been four important repercussions of this (see Rydgren 2003b; 2005): (A) it has shifted or changed the interests of certain categories of voter; (B) it has bred fears among certain voter groups (especially those to have "lost out" on the changes) that their identity is under threat; (C) it has undermined confidence in politicians in cases where the mainstream parties have been blamed for not having the power, or will, to do something about the real and perceived anomalies of the postindustrial society; and (D) it has led certain groups to feel that the cognitive frames within which they interpreted the world have become less effective, which increases the probability that they abandon old thought patterns in favor of new interpretative frames (see McAdam 1999: xxiii; cf. Swidler 1986). In the context of a decreasingly salient socioeconomic cleavage dimension, fewer people will regard political and social realities through the filter of social class. To those who have diminished in status as a consequence of the structural changes, conceptual figures that pit immigrants against "natives" (as in, "They steal our jobs") will function as an alternative interpretative framework. The combined impact, therefore, of these change processes is a situation in which more voters have been prepared to re-examine old party loyalties (owing to new interests, identities, and preferences) and look toward new parties. It could also be maintained that the changes helped to create a potential for political entrepreneurs to mobilize voters by articulating a latent authoritarianism in public opinion (by offering alternative conceptual frames with which to interpret an existence that is seen as unjust—i.e., *injustice frames*) and fuelling a latent displeasure with how parties and politicians handle postindustrial anomalies, such as high structural unemployment and an increasing unstable labor market (particularly for unskilled and low-educated voters). Studies also demonstrate that political skepticism has increased in Europe over the past few decades in step with a decline in the relative number of voters who identify with a particular party (Putnam et al. 2000). This has freed up resources for new parties to use.

(2) As we saw above, processes of dealignment and realignment can thus create favorable political opportunity structures for new parties. *Dealignment* denotes the process whereby old structural principles lose their hold on the voters, who abandon their former political loyalties (cf. Rose & McAllister 1990: 15), and *realignment* the process whereby the voting behavior of certain groups is restructured according to a new set of principles (like when the sociocultural cleavage dimension appropriates parts of the socioeconomic cleavage dimension's structuring powers).[1]

As hinted at in the opening passages of the Introduction, there is always a coexistence of parallel cleavage dimensions (see Lipset & Rokkan 1967; Rokkan 1970), the majority of which are based fundamentally on interests or social identity. Even though such cleavage dimensions exist side by side, in either latent or manifest form, their significance and political importance varies with time (see Hout et al. 1996: 55f). As mentioned in the introduction, modern Western European democracies embody two primary cleavage dimensions: the socioeconomic, which pits workers against capital (and which fundamentally concerns the size of the state's role in the economy) and the sociocultural, which pits cultural liberal values against authoritarian or particularistic values on issues such as immigration, citizenship, the family, law and order, and the like (see also Bell 1996: 332f).

Even though the sociocultural dimension has been represented in politics throughout the twentieth century, the socioeconomic cleavage dimension has structured most political behavior—not least voting behavior—in the postwar era (see Budge & Robertson 1987). However, there are certain indications that the salience of the sociocultural cleavage dimension has increased at the expense of the economic cleavage dimension during the past few decades, in many Western European countries, not least because of the politicization of political issues such as immigration, multiculturalism, feminism, and the environment (see Betz 1994, Clark & Lipset 2001; Ignazi 1996; Ingelhart 1997; Kitschelt 1995; Perrineau 1997; and Rydgren 2003b for a broader discussion and empirical indicators).

This trend has created favorable political opportunity structures for new parties—green parties and emergent far right parties alike. One can also suppose that the relative strength and importance of the dominant cleavage dimension (in this case the socioeconomic cleavage dimension) affects the possibilities of mobilizing voters around political issues and frames that belong to alternative cleavage dimensions (Kriesi et al. 1995; Schattschneider 1975). Despite the fact that anti-immigrant or xenophobic attitudes can be equally common in countries whose political systems are heavily dominated by the socioeconomic cleavage dimension (for example), the voters who share such attitudes are less inclined to choose a party in accordance with this very attitude, in that there are other issues (and attitudes) that are seen as more important. This is especially noticeable when considering the growth of the RRP parties. Since the 1990s, one characteristic feature of these political parties is their capacity to mobilize working-class voters (see e.g., Rydgren 2003b; 2004a; Mayer 1999). This has little, if anything, to do with a growing xenophobia of the working classes, and a lot to do with the increased salience of the immigration question and with the sociocultural cleavage dimension generally (in relation to issues relating to the socioeconomic cleavage dimension). Even though working-class voters have traditionally taken a more authoritarian line on sociocultural matters than the parties on which they have placed their votes (i.e., Social Democratic and Communist parties), this had little effect on their voting behavior as long as they identified themselves closely with the socialist parties' socioeconomic policies (i.e., as long as they saw these parties as defenders of their own class interests). As long as this was the case, the working classes chiefly voted for the socialist parties, their cultural liberal position on sociocultural issues notwithstanding (see Lipset 1981). However, in the political systems where the salience of the socioeconomic cleavage dimension has begun to wane, this is no longer necessarily so.

In this way, processes of realignment have been critical in shaping developments. The probability that a (radical) right-wing populist party will emerge is presumably greater in countries where the salience of the socioeconomic cleavage dimension has decreased, and where the salience of the sociocultural cleavage dimension has increased. However, processes of dealignment are also central to our understanding of the rise of new parties. Such factors include greater political alienation among certain groups of the electorate, diminished trust in political institutions (and with it a growing distrust of politicians and political parties), a decline in the number of voters with strong party identities and loyalties, and less class-based voting. Such trends are salient in a good number of Western European countries (see e.g., Putnam et al. 2000; Clark & Lipset 2001), and four prime reasons can be identified as to why this is the case: (A) The political parties and other political institutions have found it difficult to adapt to the profound economic and social changes, which have left many voters feeling that both the politics and the politicians are decoupled from the "reality" that "ordinary people" live (Mény & Surel 2000: 24), (B) The increasing complexity of the political process, combined with the declining political autonomy of the nation-state, has made the political decision-making processes more opaque and made it difficult to identify a clear power base (see Poggi 1990; Sassen 1996), (C) The real or perceived convergence between the mainstream parties in the political space, in some countries, has caused a widespread feeling that no real differences exist between the political Right and Left, that is, that there are "no real alternatives," (D) There is disillusionment of the voters in certain countries in the face of political scandals and "affairs." This coincides to a certain extent with the more aggressive tone of modern political journalism.

(3) When political parties try to mobilize issue voters, they do not only (or mainly) try to do so by attacking each other's policies but by trying to turn public (and media) attention to their favorite or profile issues (see Budge & Farlie 1983). Each party has a number of pet issues (e.g., in Sweden this would be "welfare" for the Social Democrats and "taxes" for the Conservative Party), and they go to considerable effort to make sure these issues dominate the election campaigns. Consequently, a politicization of new political issues can be closely related to the rise of new parties. The politicization of the immigration question has given the RRP parties greatly expanded political opportunity structures, partly as it has often created a niche on the voter arena (in cases where no other party has profiled itself as being staunchly anti-immigration) and partly because it has often led to greater political exposure for these parties.

However, the politicization of other issues (such as the EU or EMU) can also have an impact. It can either weaken the bonds of allegiance for otherwise loyal voters who do not share "their" party's particular views on the matter, or give new parties (such as RRP parties) a chance to broadcast their main political message by linking it to the new agenda (see Rydgren 2003a). Such a strategy can thus give the parties more media coverage.

It should also be pointed out that liberal changes to immigrant and asylum policies (for example) and a greater mobilization of political groups promoting multiculturalism can also help to expand the political opportunity structures for (radical) right-wing populist parties. Such events might mobilize voters with immigrant-skeptic or latent xenophobic attitudes, who might see their interests and/or identities in jeopardy, or they can heighten the political significance of the immigration issue in general (relative to other political issues) for voting behavior, which can benefit advocates and opponents of the multicultural society in equal measure.

(4) The degree of convergence in political space can also affect the political opportunity structure for emerging parties (see Kitschelt 1994b; 1995). Such a convergence can fuel political distrust and alienation by aggravating the feeling that there are no significant and relevant differences between the parties, and in so doing create an atmosphere in which political discontent can be articulated and mobilized (protest voting). It can also help to create niches in the voter arena. Equally important is that it can trigger the *de*politicization of a formerly dominant cleavage dimension, such as the socioeconomic dimension (see Schattschnieder 1975; Rydgren 2005), because of making it less engaging and vivid for the voters and the media, and thus becoming, in their eyes at least, less relevant. In its place a new, alternative cleavage dimension (such as the sociocultural) can then flourish, which in turn can benefit the rise of a new political party.

(5) The degree of closure or openness of a political system can also greatly affect the establishment chances of new parties. This could be a matter of whether the election system in question is one of proportional representation or "first-past-the-post" majority system, and of how high the electoral thresholds are (see Katz 1980; Weaver & Rockman 1993). The way that majority systems impede the emergence of new parties has already been noted by Duverger (1954). According to what has become known as Duverger's law, the majority system naturally leads to the rise of a relatively stable two-party political system, while a proportional representation system encourages a multiparty political system (Duverger 1954: 217). There are two reasons for this: (A) the mechanical effect of how the third or fourth largest party in a majority system receives decidedly fewer seats than would be proportionate to the number of votes cast for them; and (B) the psychological effect of the way many voters feel that a vote for a small party is a wasted vote in that the party has no real political power anyway. For obvious reasons, the chances of new parties being able to establish themselves are thus much smaller. The level at which the electoral thresholds

are set (which is 4 percent—generally—in Sweden) can also be said
to have similar mechanical and psychological effects, which means
that any chances new parties have of growing are indirectly proportional to the threshold level.

(6) The decision by one or more of the mainstream parties or other actors on the political field to work together (on any level) with the
emerging (radical) right-wing populist parties can have a profound
impact on the likelihood of its achieving an electoral breakthrough.
This is because such collaboration can legitimize the party in the
eyes of the voters (which is extremely important for marginalized
extremist parties) and give it, through the media attention thus attracted, greater political visibility (see Rydgren 2003a). Similarly,
whenever mainstream parties appropriate the policy ideas held by
the emerging party or adopt a similar political language, they are
also contributing to their legitimization.

It should, however, be noted that this can conflict with two of
the other opportunity structures discussed above, namely 1 and 4.
After all, any collaboration between one or more mainstream parties and the emerging (radical) right-wing populist party can serve
to shrink the niches available for continued mobilization on the
electoral arena (see Rydgren 2005). Such collaboration might also
hamper the emerging party in its use of the first part of the populist
antiestablishment strategy: to present itself, with some credibility, as
the only genuine opposition to the entire "political class." These different mechanisms must therefore be carefully weighed against each
other. I would suggest that a working partnership with established
parties creates favorable opportunity structures for an emerging
(radical) right-wing populist party (A) at the start of the mobilization
process (i.e., before the party has made its electoral breakthrough
on a national level), and (B) for RRP parties that have their roots in
extraparliamentary right-wing extremism. In such cases, the necessity of reducing electoral stigmatization by increasing legitimacy can
be well worth the price that possibly has to be paid for shrinking
niches on the political arena. Yet for (radical) right-wing populist
parties with their roots in populist protest movements or that lack
any kind of history at all, and for established (radical) right-wing
populist parties, collaboration with mainstream parties can actually
encumber opportunities for electoral mobilization.

Timing plays a similarly decisive role in determining whether a
situation in which the mainstream parties adopt similar policies to
the RRP parties is to the latter's advantage or not. We might expect

such ideological convergence to stunt the growth of RRP parties when it happens *before* an RRP party has made their electoral breakthrough at a national scale, but to obstruct the electoral mobilization of such parties *after* they have taken up position on the political playing field. This phenomenon is attributable both to legitimacy gains and to the possibility that voters "prefer the original to the copy."

(7) Finally, the supply of effective strategies and ideological/rhetorical profiles that resonate with the available niches on the political arena is also an influential factor. The opportunity structures discussed above lead to the emergence of successful RRP parties only if parties or embryonic political groups have the capacity to take advantage of them. In other words, a new party does not arise automatically simply because the circumstances may be ripe. Even if such strategies or ideological/rhetorical profiles are "contrived" within the emerging party from time to time, it is more common for such a party to exploit extant strategies and ideological/rhetorical profiles (especially what are referred to as *master frames*; see Rydgren 2005; Snow & Benford 1992) that they "borrow" from established parties and organizations (national or foreign). This is also why this point can be treated as part of the (external) opportunity structure rather than just as an internal resource. Previous studies (Soule 1998; McAdam & Rucht 1993; Rydgren 2004a) indicate that new, emergent parties (or social movements) primarily allow themselves to be inspired by others that (A) have proved successful, (B) have relatively close geographical propinquity, and (C) they identify with. This means that the growth of (radical) right-wing populist parties can partly be seen as an expression of cross-national diffusion processes. In the case of the tax-populist parties, the Danish Progress Party (formed by Mogens Glistrup) embarked on such a process of diffusion when it inspired political actors and emerging parties to adopt similar ideological/rhetorical profiles. In Norway such a party (Anders Lange's party, which later became the Norwegian Progress Party) was successful; in Sweden, however, the various pretenders (first and foremost the Swedish Progress Party) met with failure. The diffusion process confined itself to the Scandinavian countries. If we look at the growth of the RRP parties, we can see that a process of diffusion (that went on to encompass the whole of Western Europe) was triggered by the electoral breakthrough of the French Front National in 1984. This was the first party to succeed in uniting the "modernized" far right (with ethnonationalist xenophobia, based on the ethnopluralist doctrine, as its primary ideological

and rhetorical profile) with the populist antiestablishment strategy. When this proved successful, other emerging parties (as well as existing but politically marginalized parties) were inspired to adopt similar profiles (Rydgren 2005).

It should be stressed, however, that simply becoming a carbon copy of a successful party is generally no recipe for success, even if the political opportunity structures are favorable. The emerging party must first modify its ideological/rhetorical profile to harmonize it with the political and cultural context within which its own country's party system operates. Just how successful this modification process proves will hinge, to a certain extent at least, on the party's internal organization—which we will now discuss below.

Party organization and internal resources

Whether or not new parties emerge is, then, not simply due to the adorability of political opportunity structures; it is also a matter of how well the parties themselves manage to exploit the opportunities that present themselves. It is not only their ideological/rhetorical profiles that are critical here, but also the structure of their internal organizations and the available internal resources. The ability of a political party—and this does not only apply to RRP parties—to follow a changing public opinion and adopt new ideological/rhetorical profiles is generally more or less restricted by its own historical background and the preference of its members.

In that political parties have two principal goals—to survive as organizations and maximize their influence over the politics pursued in the given political system—they are obliged to deal with factors that occasionally curb their powers of voter maximization. First, they have to act in a way that does not undermine the cohesion of the party organization and its members' willingness to do vital yet unpaid party work. A political party with weak internal solidity is unable to maintain full control over the image given of the party by the pronouncements of individual party representatives. Second, such a party can also find it hard to compel its parliamentary group to vote in accordance with the party line on key issues. These effects can be seriously detrimental to a party's survival. Finally, a party needs a certain number of active members, partly to be able to fill any empty seats in the parliament and local government offices with able and reliable party representatives (Strøm 1990: 575), and partly to do the voluntary campaigning—which is particularly important before a party has become established (and won seats in the parliament). Without this critical mass of loyal volunteers on hand to distribute leaflets, put up posters, or give out voting slips during elections, most political parties would find themselves in difficulties (cf. Gamson 1975: 60).[2] The political parties thus still require a member organization. The problem, however, is that the factors and strategies that foster a strong, united party organization have the potential to restrict their capacity to maximize voter support (see Sjöblom 1968; Rydgren 2003b: chap. 1); this for reasons discussed below.

Party members are not politically neutral; they identify with the party ideology, with different policies, or with particular party leaders (Sjöblom 1968: 187f). This means that any attempt by the party executive to modify certain aspects of the political program can meet with resistance from the party organization. Proposed changes may generally not depart too radically from the party line already embarked upon, without a great deal of hard, time-consuming work to win the acceptance and approval among the organization; otherwise party unity is jeopardized or, at worst, disintegrates into opposing factions. However, this builds considerable party inertia, which can give rise to niches in the political arena (in cases where public opinion changes more quickly than the parties can keep up with). In some situations, it is almost impossible to anchor proposals on political change, and because of this, permanent niches can be formed.

As we can see, then, political parties can easily find themselves in situations in which the advantages of maintaining strong party unity must be weighed against the advantages of following the changing public opinion or of otherwise exploiting the potential to maximize voter support (Rose & Mackie 1988: 540; see also Lawson 1994). This mechanism not only explains the materialization of niches on the political arena but also helps us understand why emerging (radical) right-wing populist parties sometimes fail to exploit what would otherwise seem a favorable political opportunity structure for voter mobilization. Apart from this, there is above all a general problem for social movements[3] that have been transformed into political parties: while committed activists are the foremost resource for social movements, too many and too committed party members can actually pose a problem for political parties (Ahrne & Papakosta 2003), for whom the voter is the first resource of mobilization (see Rucht 1996: 187). As we have seen, the populist antiestablishment strategy was one of the most important tools for emerging right-wing populist parties. In using this strategy, the party must be able to neutralize, in a credible way, radical members of the organization who push for an uncompromising, radical party line (which in the eyes of the voters might seem overly extreme and/or antidemocratic). Not all these parties will succeed in doing this, particularly those that have their roots in extraparliamentary right-wing extremism—such as the Sweden Democrats or the French Front National—and those that have scant access to alternative resources (such as governmental party support, external sponsors, and the media) and are therefore more dependent on volunteers. One possible way of dealing with such crisis points, and this applies to mainstream and emerging RRP parties alike, is to apply one rhetoric to the "front stage" (i.e., the voters), and another to the "back stage" (i.e., the party members) (cf. Goffman 1959). However, such evasive action does not always prove effective.

Another obstacle to the ability of the mainstream parties, and to a lesser extent the right-wing populist parties, to maximize voter support is the expectations of internal party democracy. This is generally supported by the party members and is powerfully legitimizing (within most democracies). Political parties that forego at least a rudimentary internal democracy are considered illegitimate, both by the voters and by their own members (cf. Meyer & Rowan 1981; Rydgren 2003b). At the same time, a rigidly hierarchical organization makes it easier for the party leaders to follow a changing popular opinion than does a flat organization with a well-developed internal democracy. A centralized power structure can also help to solve the problem of how to deal with the real or potential internal conflicts that are a natural part of a party organization (Gamson 1975: 93, 99f). This too often forces mainstream parties to choose between legitimacy and party unity on the one hand and effectiveness and voter maximization on the other. By the inertia this trade-off situation creates, it contributes to the emergence of niches on the political arena.

The goal of maximizing influence over political decisions made by parliament can, paradoxically enough, also limit a party's powers of voter maximization (see Sjöblom 1968: 254; Rydgren 2003b: chap. 1). When the political party in question can not expect to secure a parliamentary majority, which has been the case in Sweden over the course of the period dealt with in this book, as well as in all other proportionally representative parliaments throughout Western Europe, it has little choice but to join forces (formally or informally) with other parties in order to realize as many of its political proposals as possible. However, this means that a certain degree of consideration must be paid to current or likely political partners when such a party is broadcasting its political message, and this can limit its ability to establish a political profile or to make abrupt changes in political direction. As Zald and Ash (1966: 335) have shown, for instance, political coalitions and collaborations require a certain measure of ideological compatibility. This poses little problem for *newly formed* (radical) right-wing populist parties without parliamentary representation, and for parties that have been excluded from political partnerships with established parties (either through dissociation from the other parties, or through a deliberate choice to hold the balance of power). Right-wing populist parties that have won national parliamentary representation can, however, find themselves hampered by the same strategic dilemma, which can hit them extra hard owing to the difficulties they thus face in continuing to use the populist antiestablishment strategy with any credibility.

In closing, we can conclude then that (1) political parties are encumbered by an inherent inertia, which can help to open up niches on the political arena; (2) newly formed parties, without a party history, can be at an advantage on this arena as the potential conflict between the internal arena and that of the electorate is less obvious—particularly if they have (3) a hierarchical or even authoritarian party structure, and (4) access to external resources (i.e., money and/or the media), which lessen the dependency on party members.

Nonetheless, and as we will see when discussing the collapse of New Democracy, these advantages can eventually become disadvantages, such as when the new party's membership suddenly increases dramatically as a result of an electoral breakthrough; when access to external resources declines; and/or when there are no internal democratic tools to handle splits and conflicts within the party organization.

How new right-wing populist parties emerge: a summary

Before proceeding to the empirical part of the book, let us briefly recapitulate the explanatory models sketched above. The conditions required for a new (radical) right-wing populist party to emerge and achieve an electoral breakthrough are as follows: (1) there must be favorable opportunity structures; (2) the emerging party must be able to establish an ideological/rhetorical profile to match the available niches; and (3) the emerging party must have adequate resources and a party organization sufficiently adapted to flaunt such a profile—and possibly most importantly, to make it visible—in a convincing and credible manner.

(1) Some but not all of the following political opportunity structures must be present if a (radical) right-wing populist party would emerge and establish itself nationally:

   (a) The presence of niches available on the voter arena, defined as a given demand (from the electorate) that is not satisfied by a corresponding supply (from the mainstream parties). There must also be a sufficient number of floating voters (i.e., those with a relatively low degree of party identification). We may assume that the emergence of tax populism largely depended on niches on the right of the socioeconomic cleavage dimension combined with widespread tax discontent; for the RRP parties, on the other hand, niches to the right of the sociocultural cleavage dimension (mainly immigration but also "law and order") were critical to their evolution.

(b) Dealignment and Realignment. Opportunities for emerging (radical) right-wing populist parties generally increase when more voters abandon their old party loyalties (dealignment) and, at least in the case of the RRP parties, when the sociocultural cleavage dimension increases in political salience at the expense of the socioeconomic cleavage dimension (realignment).

(c) The politicization of new issues. The politicization of immigration in the 1980s and 1990s was of particular importance, especially for the emergence of RRP parties. Other issues that cut straight across established party lines were also key factors (e.g., the EU question).

(d) Convergence in political space. The opportunities for new parties to locate available resources diminish in political systems in which the mainstream parties are dispersed over the entire spectrum.

(e) An electoral system based on proportional representation with relatively low electoral thresholds benefits new parties. Even if this factor is normally unable to explain changes in degree of mobilization over time within any one political system, it may help us understand differences between countries.

(f) The decision by mainstream parties to collaborate with the emerging right-wing populist parties can be both an advantage and a disadvantage. When the new party has its roots in extraparliamentary right-wing extremism it is mainly a positive thing for the party owing to its legitimizing effects; when the new party has its roots in a populist protest movement, we can expect it to be mainly a negative thing for the party owing to shrinking niches on the voter arena.

(g) Access to suitable strategies and ideological/rhetorical profiles (within the party or, more often, with extant parties of a similar nature) that the parties can use to derive political benefit from whatever favorable opportunity structures might exist. The populist antiestablishment strategy had a critical role to play here for both the tax populist parties and the RRP parties, as, in the case of the latter, did the ethnopluralist doctrine (despite the significance of other rhetorical strategies, such as "welfare chauvinism").

How successful emerging right-wing populist parties have been in exploiting any openings for voter mobilization depends to great extent on their access to internal resources and their organizational structures. Too great a dependence on voluntary party activists can create problems for such parties, particularly if the members identify with a political line that is considered too extremist by the public. In such cases, the emerging party will have difficulties in applying the populist antiestablishment strategy with any genuine credibility.

Notes

1. My use of the term leaves it open as to whether or not the structuring power of the new cleavage dimension is based on emergent *new* loyalties. In this sense, my use of the term is more behavioral than it is social psychological.
2. This also applies though the need for such internal (labor intensive) resources has declined somewhat since the advent of television and the media society (cf. Epstein 1967; McCarthy & Zald 1977). Much of the process of electoral mobilization takes place today through public channels, while labor-intensive campaign work such as knocking on doors has become relatively rare (see Snow et al. 1980: 790; for Sweden, see Esaiasson 1990), even though members can still be used to man the faxes, computers, etc. (Scarrow 1996). The need for labor-intensive resources has, however, declined—at least for the mainstream parties—as governmental party support has increased (Strøm 1990: 575).
3. RRP parties that have not yet had their electoral breakthrough (e.g., the Sweden Democrats in the 1990s, Front National in the 1970s, and Lega Nord in the 1980s) function more as social movements than political parties (see Ruzza 2004). The Sweden Democrats and the Front National are also examples of parties that emerged out of social movements.

3

The Rise of New Democracy

While tax populist parties had already started to surface in Denmark and Norway by the early 1970s, the Swedish five-party system remained intact until the electoral breakthrough of the Green Party in 1988. The absence of a Swedish "Progress Party" on the national political arena inspired a great deal of debate, especially in light of the growing lack of confidence in politicians among the Swedish electorate at the time. One common explanation for this absence is that the nonsocialist parties had remained an untried alternative in Sweden up until 1976, leaving Swedes, unlike their Danish and Norwegian neighbors, with no experience of right-wing rule. General tax discontent and political distrust might consequently have been directed primarily at the sitting government party, which had been in power for generations (e.g., Goul Andersen & Bjørklund 1990). Goul Andersen and Bjørklund (1990) also stress the absence of referenda or other major issues that cut across established party lines and loyalties and that in so doing release floating voters. This is true insofar as no referendum on EC membership was held in Sweden during this time (whereas Denmark and Norway both appealed to the electorate in 1972, just before the electoral breakthrough of each country's Progress Party), but it overlooks the importance of the environment and nuclear power as political concerns. In the 1970s, however, much of the populist current, propelled as it was by such issues, was channeled through the Center Party, which thus became something of a surrogate populist party, draining the market of resources that otherwise might have prepared the way for a new party (Fryklund & Peterson 1981). Furthermore, as a result of the 1980 referendum on nuclear power the Green Party was founded in 1981.

It was only after 1982, after six years of nonsocialist rule, when concerns about the nonsocialist parties' failure to reduce the tax pressure had emerged and when a new political issue—immigration—had started to take hold, that tax populist voices had any kind of political impact in Sweden, albeit initially at a local level. In the south of Sweden, the Skåne Party made gains around the mid 1980s, especially in Malmö, where it reaped 7.2 percent of the votes in the 1985 local elections (Peterson et al. 1988). Two or three years later, anti-immigrant and even purely xenophobic currents manifested themselves in the Skåne town of Sjöbo when the leader of the local Center Party, Sven-Olle Olsson, arranged a referendum on whether the town should accommodate political refugees, a proposal that was rejected by a resounding majority of locals. The referendum itself, not least the way in which the campaign was fought, attracted the attention of the national media, and demonstrated the potential that anti-immigration had for electoral mobilization. Expelled from the Center Party, Olsson formed the Sjöbo Party, and after enjoying a relative measure of success in the local elections of 1988, went on to stand in the general election that same year (Fryklund & Peterson 1989).

However, a Swedish right-wing populist party did not succeed on a national level until the 1990s, when New Democracy won 6.7 percent of the vote in the 1991 general election. The official account is that its founders, Ian Wachtmeister and Bert Karlsson, met for the first time at Arlanda airport some time in the middle of November the year before.[1] Wachtmeister had apparently read in *Expressen* (a national popular tabloid) that Karlsson had appointed him prime minister in his dream-team government, and they discussed the matter while waiting for their flights. A week or so later (November 23) both appeared on television on *Svar Direkt*, during which program host Siewert Öholm announced that, according to a (specially commissioned) Sifo poll, 23 percent of the electorate could imagine voting for "Bert Karlsson's party" (Gardberg 1993: 44). This heralded the birth of Wachtmeister and Karlsson's new party, the Sifo survey having already secured it, even before its inception, a great deal of media attention. Both men were also well-known public figures: Karlsson was the director of a record label and the owner of the amusement park Skara Sommarland and had also built up something of a political reputation through his attack on food prices; Wachtmeister was a businessman (and had previously been the president of large listed companies, and he also owned the company "The Empire Inc.") and was associated with the SAF (Swedish Employers' Confederation)-supported *New Welfare* think tank. He had also written works of popular political nonfiction in which he poked fun at Swedish politicians and the Swedish bureaucracy (Taggart 1996; Westlind 1996; Wachtmeister 1988; 1990). Two days later, it was announced that the two had formed a party, whose manifesto they presented in a debate article submitted to the major national newspaper *Dagens Nyheter* (Karlsson & Wachtmeister 1990). On 1 December 1990 the party was officially given the name New Democracy, and the required list of signatures was collected to permit registration, which took place on 4 February 1991, the date of the party's formal inception.

As we will see below, the path to the election was by no means smooth for New Democracy, despite its riding the crest of a wave in the polls (the 4 percent threshold had already been passed by Sifo's first survey; see Rydgren 1996). Their first major setback occurred in February 1991, when Karlsson was invited onto the TV program *Magasinet*. He showed himself incapable of answering the occasionally complex political questions fired at him by program host Olle Stenholm, and failed to explain just *how* they were hoping to implement the party's political program. Karlsson decided to resign as a party leader, which was announced in a radio interview on the *Efter Tre* program. Nevertheless, Karlsson soon made a comeback and as we shall see, New Democracy not only was able to rescue itself from its predicament with the help of the populist antiestablishment strategy, it also managed to turn Karlsson's failure to its advantage.

The remainder of this chapter will be structured along the lines of the explanatory model presented in chapter 2. First we will be discussing the political opportunity structures available to New Democracy. Congruent with this discussion, the sociological bases and attitudinal motivations of New Democracy's voters will also be analyzed. Then we will investigate how the party, largely with the help of the populist antiestablishment strategy and an occasionally xenophobic anti-immigration and anti-immigrant stance, were able to take advantage of the opportunities available for mobilizing the voters. Finally, we will take a look at New Democracy's unique organizational structure and their alternative means of securing resources.

Political opportunity structures: neoliberalism, xenophobia, and populism

As we shall see in this and the next section, a niche opened up on the Swedish voter arena—the anti-immigrant and immigration niche within a developing sociocultural dimension—before the emergence of

New Democracy, and the party was also favored by a general shift to the right in the socioeconomic dimension and by the emergence of a pure protest dimension. As we shall also see, long-term change processes coincided with short-lived singular events to stimulate the development of these three processes just at the end of the 1980s and the early 1990s.

The significance of the anti-immigrant niche and the protest dimension will mainly be dealt with in the coming sections. For the time being, however, I shall concentrate on the importance of the shift to the right in the socioeconomic dimension. In the latter part of the 1980s, voter opinion started to shift to the right, a process that grew in strength around the turn of the decade. Traditionally speaking there have, since the Second World War, always been more voters identifying themselves with the left than with the right, a disparity that disappeared in the 1980s when the number of people on either the right or the left was fairly evenly balanced (35 percent for each side in the 1988 election, for example). However, in the 1991 election, the proportion of voters considering themselves on the "right" suddenly increased to 44 percent at the expense of the "leftists," who dropped to 27 percent (Gilljam & Holmberg 1993: 137). This swing in public opinion also becomes apparent when we look at attitudes to the welfare state: the proportion of voters who said that they would like to see a *smaller* public sector increased dramatically between 1989 and 1990 from 42 to 56 percent. Even if this discrepancy had receded somewhat by the time of the 1991 election, at which time 50 percent of the electorate advocated a reduction of the public sector with 23 percent opposed to such a policy (Nilsson 1002: 39), it is still a clear indication of the direction in which the political winds were blowing at the start of the 1990s. As Stefan Svallfors has shown, the 1980s were also marked by a jadedness or latent discontent toward the welfare state, so much so that during the latter half of the decade, some 75 percent agreed with the statement that many of those on unemployment benefits could find a job if they really wanted to. By 1996, however, once the winds had changed direction, this figure had halved (Svallfors 1989; 1997). Just how real this shift to the right was can be seen in the failure of the two left-wing parties (the Left Party and the Social Democrats) to win over any more than a meager 27 percent of first-time voters in the 1991 general election (2 and 25 percent respectively), by far the poorest performance ever (and should be compared with the 49 percent in the election of only three years previously). By contrast, the Conservative Party and New Democracy took home 44 percent of first-time votes in the 1991 election (30 percent and 14 percent respectively) (Gilljam & Holmberg 1993: 83).

This socioeconomic shift to the right was the product of several interacting factors. We should not, for instance, underestimate the fall of Communism in Eastern Europe, which led to the "triumphal advance of the market economy"; nor should we forget the impact of the powerful boom economy during the end of the 1980s. To add to this, there was the ideological offensive led by the Swedish Employers' Confederation and its information and propaganda agency, Timbro, during the 1980s. This campaign, which was inspired by the successes of the new right in the U.S.A. (Reagan) and Britain (Thatcher), was designed to break the leftist hegemony in ideological debate and agenda setting in Sweden; and as Boréus (1994; 1997) has pointed out, neoliberalism also made a clear mark on the public political discourse during the 1980s. However, it should be stressed that at the time, the Swedish "right-wing wave," unlike the continental and Anglo-Saxon, was built exclusively on neoliberalism: "neoconservatism," as it has come to be known, did not appear until the 1990s (Boréus 1997: 277).

I find it plausible that these rightist currents underpinned New Democracy's election success; nevertheless, it is not enough to explain why New Democracy was able to establish itself in the first place. The more right-wing political climate should first and foremost have benefited the extant right-wing party, the Conservative Party. As we will see below, we cannot talk of a neoliberal niche in the economic right-left dimension since the Conservative Party satisfied such a need. However, link this rightist wind to political distrust and the populist strategy, and we might begin to approach a valid reason. Because many voters were dissatisfied with the mainstream parties, they were prepared to give their votes to a completely new party. The fact that such a party was a right-wing one (New Democracy) was partly due to the rightist currents on the socioeconomic right-left dimension. We also know that 14 percent of New Democracy's voters stated that their choice of party was heavily determined by economic policy. However, this figure was exceeded by those who stated that they had been attracted to New Democracy because of its position on immigrant and refugee issues; 19 percent of the party's supporters gave this as their foremost reason for having given their vote to a particular party (Gilljam & Holmberg 1993: 95). Further, appearing alongside the right-wing wind that was blowing through the socioeconomic dimension was an anti-immigrant niche with occasional xenophobic overtones; this was also of importance, possibly (as we shall soon see) even critical to the emergence of New Democracy and its successes in the 1991 general election. Also when we look at voter attitudes, we find that issues of immigration and refugees were, along with the economy (particularly tax policies), New Democracy's greatest asset:

for example, 52 percent of those who voted for the party thought that it had a sound refugee policy (against the 3 percent who opposed it), the corresponding figures for tax policy being 35 and 2 percent (Gilljam & Holmberg 1993: 37). Moreover, twice as many people approved of New Democracy's asylum policy as voted for the party itself (13 percent of the electorate). It should therefore not be forgotten how quickly public opinion had changed on immigration and asylum: as late as 1988 voter opinion toward the acceptance of refugees was positive (i.e., those who considered it a bad idea to take in fewer refugees outnumbered those who thought it good); by 1991, the balance had tipped dramatically, and what had been a positive 6 percent was suddenly a negative 26 percent (Gilljam & Holmberg 1993: 155).

As implied above, these two factors would not have been so effective had they not coincided with a burgeoning protest dimension in Swedish politics and (and partly as a consequence of this) with a process that gave Sweden, like other Western European countries, an increasingly volatile voter arena, freeing up resources for emerging new parties. The proportion of party-defectors (i.e., people who change political loyalties between two general elections) started to rise sharply in the mid 1980s. From the late 1970s up until this time, the number of defectors had remained a fairly constant 18 or 19 percent. The 20 percent barrier was broken in the 1988 election, and by the time of the 1991 election, it had increased to no less than 30 percent (Gilljam & Holmberg 1993: 71). A growing distrust of politicians and declining party identification also helped to gradually undermine the position of the established parties and released more floating voters, available for electoral mobilization of new emerging parties. In other words, resources had been freed up on the Swedish voter arena, a development that was especially salient from the 1980s into the 1990s. There are clear indications that New Democracy managed to attract many of these floating voters; for instance, 83 percent of the party's supporters decided how to vote only after the election campaign had begun, which was significantly more than for the other parties and over 30 percent higher than the average (Gilljam & Holmberg 1993: 48).

If we take a close look at the demographic and sociological breakdown of the 1991 general election results, we find that New Democracy was very much supported by the working class (10 percent of industrial workers voted for the party) and small business proprietors (12 percent). Of its voters, 24 percent had voted for the Social Democrats in the 1988 election, 20 percent for the Conservative Party, and 18 percent had voted blank. Eleven percent had not been entitled to vote in the 1988 election (Gilljam & Holmberg 1993: 73, 199). Males, the young, and residents of rural areas and small towns were also overrepresented among New Democracy's supporters (Gilljam & Holmberg 1993: 211, 232f). However, when conducting a logistic regression analysis, which allows us to control for the effect of other relevant variables, it becomes evident that both small traders/enterprisers (in particular) and high-ranking officials were better predictors for explaining the vote on New Democracy (Table 3.1).[2] When controlling for other relevant variables, both small traders and enterprisers were about two and a half times as likely to vote for New Democracy as the reference category employees, whereas no significant association could be established between being an industrial worker and having a high likelihood for voting for New Democracy.[3]

Moreover, we learn from Table 3.1. that contrary to the contemporary RRP parties (e.g., Rydgren 2003b), poorly educated voters were not

Table 3.1. The sociology of New Democracy's voters in the 1991 Parliamentary election, logistic regression analysis

Wage income	1.000
Low education	0.932
University level education	0.440[1]
(Senior high school)	(1.000)
Industrial worker	1.571
Small traders/enterprisers	2.555[2]
High-ranking officials	2.430[2]
(Employees, officials)	(1.000)
Unemployed	0.599
(Full employed)	(1.000)
Impaired personal economy	1.652[1]
(No change in personal economy)	(1.000)
Age	0.980[1]
Gender (male)	1.374
Psedo-R2	0.053
Prob>Chi2	0.000
Log likelihood	-542.68
N	2,377

[1] *Significant on the 0.05 level.*
[2] *Significant on the 0.01 level.*

more likely to vote for New Democracy, although it could be established that very highly educated voters (i.e., voters with university-level educations) were significantly less likely to vote for the party. Furthermore, also contrary to many contemporary RRP parties (Golder 2003), unemployed voters were not more likely to vote for New Democracy.[4] In sum, this analysis indicates that New Democracy was not a result of a revolt from below in the sense that economically deprived voters turned to the party, but was rather supported by voters who were relatively well off (although income in itself failed to show a significant relationship to the likelihood to vote for the New Democracy); such as relatively high-ranked officials and the petty bourgeoisie of small traders and enterprisers. However, it might nonetheless be a partial result of a feeling of relative deprivation, since voters who had experienced an impaired personal economy during the years before the election were significantly more likely to vote for the party.[5]

Yet, when discussing the reasons for the party's growth, it should, however, be borne in mind that no less than 39 percent of those who voted for New Democracy actually sympathized with some other party but placed their vote with New Democracy for tactical reasons to make sure that the party cleared the 4 percent threshold (either in order to salvage a nonsocialist majority or to push politics in a "New Democratic" direction on one or more issues, or quite simply because they liked the idea of "breathing some fresh air" into the political system). Gilljam and Holmberg (1993: 112) estimate that the party would have teetered precariously on the threshold of 4 percent had it not been for these tactical voters.

To return to the theoretical model discussed in chapter 2, Sweden has also demonstrably undergone a macrostructural process of change in its partial transition from an industrial to a postindustrial society. For instance, the proportion of industrial workers dropped from 37 percent in 1973 to 30 percent in 1983 and again to 26 percent in 1995. During this same period, the proportion of service employees increased from 56 percent, to 65 percent and finally to 71 percent (OECD 1996: 191). Such a transition could well have helped to create favorable opportunity structures for emerging (radical) right-wing populist parties for different reasons. For example, traditional working-class environments were partly dismantled by the diminished size of the industrial sector and the growing diversification of the working class, itself caused by increased specialization and heavier demands on technical skills (see Dahrendorf 1959). An indication of this development is that while almost 90 percent of workers identified with the working class in 1950, only 50 percent did so in 1988 (Ahrne et al. 2000: 72f; Cigéhn 1990). Although this figure increased again during the 1990s, probably in response to the economic crisis and the growing class cleavages (Cigéhn 1999), it is still well below the level of 1950 (but very high nonetheless from a contemporary comparative perspective). A repercussion of this is that class voting (i.e., the proportion of workers who vote for a leftist party and the proportion of middle-class voters who vote for a nonsocialist party) has declined in Western Europe—as it did in Sweden in the decade from 1982 to 1991, when class voting among the working class fell from 70 percent to 57 percent (Gilljam & Holmberg 1993: 196; see also Nieuwbeerta 2001). Seen from an international perspective, this figure was still high and as we shall see, the impact of the class-voting factor increased once more in the 1990s. However, in the 1991 election, New Democracy benefited from a slightly disproportionately large support of working-class voters.

Greater political distrust and new political conflicts?

To quote Oscarsson (1998: 3f), "[I]n no other democratic system [have the citizens] had so little difficulty understanding similarities and differences between political alternatives and been able to see the cleavage structure so clearly as in Sweden." This is because Sweden for a very long time had a solidly one-dimensional cleavage structure, in which the economic cleavage dimension has been manifestly dominant (cf. Rokkan 1970), and because the party system has been so stable. Moreover, the economic cleavage dimension has faced no competition from linguistic, religious, or ethnic conflicts, and the only competing cleavage dimension before the 1970s was that between town and country (Bergström 1991: 8). One important reason why the socioeconomic cleavage dimension has been so resilient in Sweden compared to elsewhere is that in no other Western European country is there, or has there been, such a dominant party as the Swedish Social Democrats (see Bergström 1991).

In consequence, no new party was able to challenge the five mainstream Riksdag parties before the end of the 1980s, and (as we will see in chapter 5) no Swedish RRP party has managed to establish itself since the collapse of New Democracy in 1994. As suggested above, there are indications that the strong position of the mainstream parties was gradually undermined during the 1980s, producing a more mobile voter arena, and as already discussed, the number of party defectors increased sharply while class voting declined. Further, during the 1970s and 1980s another stabilizing factor in politics was weakening, namely party identification (i.e., the sense of affinity that a voter has with a particular party and that can be expected to influence his or her vote), so that while in 1968, 65 percent of the voters said that they felt some sort of affinity with one party or another, by 1991, this figure had decreased to 48 percent. Even voters with strong party identification showed a similarly dramatic decline, from 39 percent in 1968 to only 24 percent in 1991 (Gilljam & Holmberg 1993: 174). This helped to free up more resources in the 1980s, when the opinions held by the electorate on different political issues started to have a more profound impact on their choice of party, which in turn enabled vacant niches to appear on the voter arena. Probably even more importantly, political distrust grew noticeably over the course of this period; in 1968, 46 percent agreed with the statement, "Those who sit in the Riksdag and take decisions do not pay much attention to what ordinary people think." In 1982 it was 60 percent, and no less than 70 percent in 1991. The proportion of those who claimed to have little or very little confidence in Swedish politicians increased from 55 percent in 1988 to 61 percent in 1991 (Gilljam & Holmberg 1993: 170f). Hence, we can see how these developments had the effect of destabilizing the party system, which facilitated New Democracy's ability to mobilize voters for two reasons: by releasing resources in the form of voters who had no emotional "affiliation" with any one party; and by preparing a fertile ground for mobilizing protest voting. It is also symptomatic that New Democracy was formed at a time when the sense of uncertainty among the Swedish electorate was at its greatest. In fact, in the late autumn of 1990, pollsters Sifo and TIMO both reported that 21.2 and 20.5 percent respectively of the franchised lacked party sympathies (Gilljam & Holmberg 1993).

There are several possible causes of this mood of uncertainty and political distrust, the 1980 nuclear power referendum being a possible candidate. Referenda are rare in Sweden, and when they concern issues that cut across established party boundaries, they can weaken bonds of loyalty between the voters and the parties (see Goul Andersen & Bjørklund 1990; 2000). However, whereas the nuclear power referendum was a critical factor behind the growth of the Green Party, it was probably of only limited and indirect significance to the success of New Democracy in the 1991 general election.

Studies of Danish politics (Rydgren 2004a) also reveal that the strength of Social Democracy have a strong influence on the political stability in Scandinavian politics, and not least on the relative importance of the socioeconomic cleavage dimension: when Social Democratic parties falter, so does political stability and the relative importance of the socioeconomic dimension. (However, the problem is that the causal relation can be the converse, so we must remain receptive to the historical context.) It is thus of relevance to note that Swedish Social

Democracy encountered a number of problems at the end of the 1980s and the early 1990s, on both the parliamentary and internal arenas. First, the Social Democrat party fell into difficulties handling the issue of collective wage-earners' funds, a socialist measure designed to give wage-earners strong representation in the boards of business corporations, which was something that engaged the unions and many party members but apparently left the party leadership somewhat cold (and the proposal became increasingly watered down with the passing of time). Second, the Social Democrat government was "forced" to abandon a number of its earlier profile issues; this was seen as a step to the right, and it led to what came to be called "the War of the Roses" between the right (reformists) and the left (traditionalists) flanks of the party movement. The Swedish economy became all the more strained at the turn of the decade, compelling the Social Democrat government to impose a series of unpopular measures. In 1989 they called for an increase in VAT, which led, however, to an agreement with the Center Party on "compulsory saving," a program that also failed to gain a great deal of acceptance from the voters. In February of the following year, the Government delivered a radical plan of action that included a proposal for a temporary ban on strikes and for frozen wage levels, and that provoked an outcry among the Social Democratic Party organization. When the Government failed to win majority backing for its action package, Social Democratic Prime Minister Ingvar Carlsson and his party resigned from power, only to return a few days later, without, that is, Finance Minister Kjell-Olof Feldt. In April of 1990, the Government reached an agreement with the Liberal Party by which it refrained from implementing its election promises from the 1988 campaign and introduced qualifying days into the health insurance system (Bergström 1991: 15f). Support for the Social Democrats declined rapidly and by early 1991 had reached as low as 30 percent (Sainsbury 1992: 161). On top of this, the Social Democrat Party performed a U-turn on EC membership and applied to join the European Community in July 1991. To make matters worse for the party, just prior to the election in September 1991 Kjell-Olof Feldt published his memoirs, in which he denounced the sitting government and declared the politics of the "Swedish third way" no longer legitimate (Sainsbury 1992: 162). Apart from the potential damage this inflicted on the Social Democrats, especially as it provided the nonsocialist parties with choice quotes for the televised election debates as well as proof in black-and-white of their opponent's internal rifts, it also created a feeling that Swedish social democracy was ideologically disillusioned and that the old established political interpretive frames had grown weak and impotent.[6]

That New Democracy benefited not only from the greater uncertainty and mobility of the voters but also from this mounting political distrust is demonstrated by the fact that no less than 53 percent of those who voted for the party justified their choice by citing the need for "fresh new approaches" and for "shaking things up," and by claiming that the party spoke the mind of the man in the street (Gilljam & Holmberg 1993: 90). We also know that a massive 79 percent of New Democracy's voters admitted to having little confidence (very or fairly) in Swedish politicians, by far the highest degree of political discontent of the entire electorate (excluding blank voters but including abstainers) (Gilljam & Holmberg 1993: 173). As we will see below, variables measuring political discontent and frustration were also among the most important attitudinal factors for predicting why some voters rather than others decided to vote for New Democracy.

So far we have seen that at the time of New Democracy's rise, resources had been freed up in the form of "party disloyal" voters and a protest dimension in Swedish politics had been established alongside a right-shift on the economic cleavage dimension. These processes combined to create favorable opportunity structures for a party such as New Democracy. Finally, we can add that an anti-immigration/anti-immigrant niche had been exposed, which very much coincided with the politicization of the immigrant/refugee question (which we will be discussing later). In the 1991 election, the contours of an alternative cleavage dimension began to surface; they returned to a state of latency for the rest of the decade, only to appear manifest again for the 2002 election, as we will see in coming chapters. This cleavage dimension between xenophobia and cosmopolitanism, between the "open" and "closed" society, can be seen as a component of the more general sociocultural cleavage dimension, which has been central to the growth and establishment of RRP parties throughout Western Europe.

In the late 1980s and early 1990s, the Swedish electorate grew more hostile toward the accommodation of refugees, asylum, and development aid, and the immigration issue became an increasing political concern for many voters (Gilljam & Holmberg 1993). At the same time, all mainstream parties were more or less in agreement that Sweden would continue to accept refugees, even if their immigration and integration policies were at variance with each other. All this exposed a niche in which a party of immigrant and immigration skeptics could attract voters. Postelection surveys also showed that New Democracy voters occupied an extreme position on the xenophobic flank of the electorate, scoring an average of 27 on an additive index ranging from 0 (rejecting the proposal to increase immigrant support, advocating the reduction of development aid and the accommodation of fewer asylum-seekers) to 100 (advocating the proposal to increase immigrant support, rejecting the reduction of development aid and the accommodation of fewer asylum-seekers). In comparison, Conservative Party voters scored 37, Center Party voters 44, Social Democrat voters 47, Christian Democrat voters 51, Liberal Party voters 52, Left Party voters 60, and Green Party voters 68 (Gilljam & Holmberg 1993: 157). As we will see below, voters critical or skeptical of refugee immigration and state-supported aid to developing countries, as well as those who considered the immigration issue as being of high salience, were considerably more likely to vote for New Democracy.

The politicization and greater significance of immigration

For many years, Swedish immigration policy enjoyed remarkable political consensus. For example, all Riksdag parties supported the decision in 1975 to initiate a Swedish immigration policy (Södergran 2000: 7ff), and even if the Left Party and, to a lesser extent, the Liberal Party started to initiate parliamentary debates on asylum and immigration policies in the early 1980s, these were not issues that galvanized the public in any great way. Not, that is, before 1987 (Demker 1993: 146), a year after the 1986 parliamentary resolution on new immigrant policy guidelines, which marked the start of the visible disintegration of this consensus—although the disunity did not manifest itself fully until the 1989 resolution on a new Aliens Act, when the Social Democrat government took the initiative on a resolution regarding temporary ceilings on asylum figures. In Södergran's (2000: 9) words, "Immigration, asylum and immigration policy issues . . . generally became the more frequent subject of discussion. Many debates were split as regards the merits and defects of immigration policy (not to mention policy predictions of immigration's effects) and the number of reservations on political decisions rose dramatically"—no less than fifty for the 1989 Riksdag resolution (Södergran 1998: 27), for instance. Much of the growing disagreement on asylum and immigration policy took the form of condemnation of the government, which many thought intent on imposing a too-strict immigration policy. One decision to elicit such disapproval, and that many interpreted as an indication of an ever more stringent asylum policy, was that made in January 1990 to deport 5,000 Turkish Bulgarians, which the Government justified by citing a report from a Swedish delegation that their fears of facing trial (for political reasons) when returning to Turkey "were largely unfounded" (Arter 1992: 359).

However, anti-immigrant voices, already critical of what they considered an overly generous immigration policy, also started to make themselves more heard. The events in Sjöbo in 1988 (see above) also had a key role to play in these developments as they not only articulated a latent public discontent, but also demonstrated to political actors that it was possible to make electoral gains also in Sweden with an anti-immigrant and anti-immigration message tinted with xenophobic overtones. The fact that these sentiments became more salient across Sweden at the time they did (the latter half of the 1980s) was probably a response not just to the greater number of refugees entering the country at the time but also to the Government decision of 1985 regarding the "Sweden-wide program" to disperse asylum seekers around the entire country (see, e.g., Södergran 2000). As a consequence, small towns that had had no previous contact with non-Scandinavian immigrants (via previous refugee immigration or the labor immigration of the 1960s from countries like Yugoslavia and Turkey) were now finding themselves having to deal directly and regularly with people from different cultural areas. This made the refugee issue more tangible and politically acute for many voters. But we can also speculate whether the more austere asylum policy of the late 1980s was seen by many as an admission that the country had already taken in too many refugees: why would the Government otherwise impose limits?

New Democracy was thus not the first to break the Swedish consensus by criticizing Swedish immigration policy, even if it was one of the first to do so in overtly xenophobic terms on a national scale. Yet even before the party was founded, public opinion was ripe, and at the time New Democracy was formed, more Swedes than ever before (61 percent) believed that the country was taking in too many immigrants (Gardberg 1992: 50, Demker 2000: 74). In the general election of 1991, 8 percent of voters also claimed that the issue of asylum and immigration strongly influenced their choice of party as opposed to 1 percent in the 1985 general election and 2 percent in 1988 (Holmberg 2000: 114).

Convergence in political space

Although a convergence in political space (i.e., when the policies of two or more of the major mainstream parties approach each other) took place in Sweden before the rise of New Democracy, it was probably of no benefit to the party, as it mainly represented a shift to the right. As mentioned above, the Social Democrats gradually began to abandon their traditional policies at this time. During the latter half of the 1980s, not only did they embark on a deregulation of the financial market and changing of the tax system, they also started to turn the focus away from full employment toward low inflation, privatizing the utilities, and abolishing the TV and radio monopolies (Kitschelt 1994a). In other words, it too took a step to the right along the economic dimension, a shift to the right that was also noted by the voters, who, when invited to place the party on a ten-point scale from 0 (far left) to 10 (far right), gave it a score of 3.5 during the 1991 general election, up from 2.8 in 1985 and 3.2 in 1988. The Conservative Party, meanwhile, retained its position on the far right, even if the party was considered to have migrated to the left from the mid 1980s onward (from a score of 9.0 in the 1985 general election to 8.7 in that of 1991). New Democracy ended up at 8.0 on the scale in the 1991 election, somewhat to the left of the Conservative Party (Holmberg 2000: 124). This might be a reflection of how the party's populist profile concealed its neoliberal agenda. Whatever the case, it is clear that the rise of New Democracy cannot be considered the product of political convergence; rather, the party succeeded *despite* the fact that the Conservative Party was already seen as a distinct right-wing alternative by the voters.

Naturally, it is possible to interpret the relative consensus on the asylum and immigration questions as reflecting a convergence in an alternative cleavage dimension, and here there can be no doubt that New Democracy took advantage of a vacant niche.

A relatively open political system

The Swedish political system, based as it is on proportional representation, is a relatively open one despite the fact that the purely political thresholds (of 4 percent) are twice as high as in Denmark. As these thresholds were the same for the election of 1991, the rise of New Democracy can scarcely be considered the product of changes in the mechanical effect identified by Duverger (see chapter 2). At the same time, we should not forget that New Democracy passed the 4 percent threshold by a wide margin in Sifo's survey taken back in February 1991, and by April the party was scoring no less than 11.7 percent. Although the party declined somewhat in the polls as the election approached, it was still far over 4 percent (see Rydgren 1996). Presumably, then, the psychological effect that potentially deters people from voting for new parties was somewhat mitigated, while the figures the party was scoring in the polls helped allay concerns that a vote for New Democracy would be a wasted vote. At the same time we should be careful not to overestimate the importance of this mechanism, as we know that the popularity of the Green Party as suggested by polls taken in April 1982 (when it reached 7 percent) did not help the party win a single seat in the general election later that year (Vedung 1988).

Alongside these purely political thresholds, we can also identify a "media threshold" and a "funding threshold," both of which encumber the rise of new parties (Vedung 1988). If a new party is excluded from the media coverage, the chances of its disseminating any message are severely limited. An important example of such a "media threshold" is that by tradition, Swedish public service television only allows parties with parliamentary seats to take part in televised debates, occasions that considerably influence the outcome of general elections. In 1991, however, Swedish television changed the rules on which parties were allowed to participate in the major party leader debates, and decided to allow in New Democracy—partly in recognition of the considerable attention that the party had attracted in the political discourse and partly owing to the high figures they were receiving in the polls (Gilljam & Holmberg 1993: 16).[7] Both the Conservative Party and the Social Democrats tried in vain to oppose the decision (see Westlind 1996: 163). However, their opposition was exploited by New Democracy, which accused them (as well as the media in general) of being undemocratic in their unwillingness to give all parties equal exposure (Westlind 1996: 163). It should also be remembered that this "media threshold" was at its most effective when state-run Swedish Television had a broadcasting monopoly. With the appearance of new TV channels and formats (in which politicians appear as much on light entertainment programs as on political panel debates) over the past fifteen years, the effects of this mechanism have greatly diminished. The party also managed to gain powerful media attention from day one, not least owing to Wachtmeister and Karlsson's established fame. Although its status as a media darling waned as time passed, New Democracy was a typical "media party" nonetheless, one that was constantly much more heavily dependent on disseminating its message via media channels than on its party members (cf. Gardberg 1993: 44).

Finally, the "funding threshold" comprises the principle that Swedish party subsidies are geared to election results, which means that only the relatively well established parties receive financial support (Vedung 1988). Consequently, it is hard for a newly formed party, with its limited resources, to afford campaign material, printed ballot papers for all polling stations, and so on, and this severely hampers voter mobilization. As we shall see, however, New Democracy managed to make use of alternative resources, thus mitigating the effect of this particular threshold.

Relations with the mainstream parties: mutual disassociation or legitimizing contact?

The reaction of the mainstream parties to the rise of New Democracy was initially one of wariness. Apart from the Liberal Party and its leader Bengt Westerberg, which relatively early on pronounced the party something of an arch-enemy in the election campaign and which repeatedly denounced its xenophobia (even pledging during the election campaign to refuse to collaborate with a government dependent on the support of New Democracy, a promise that it nevertheless later reneged on), there was a general tendency to avoid direct debate and confrontation with New Democracy. Rather than face this new political force, the mainstream parties tried to deprive it of even more political and media attention by simply ignoring it (Widfeldt 2004). Whether this damaged or bolstered New Democracy is hard to say; on the one hand it was offered no further publicity, but on the other it might well have made it easier for the party to successfully use its antiestablishment strategy, allowing the two leaders to accuse the mainstream parties of not deigning to listen to "the common man" (whose opinions New Democracy claimed to champion). However, as the party was not stigmatized as antidemocratic, and newly formed to boot, there was no pressing need of greater legitimacy.

Contact with and influences from similar parties

New Democracy denied fervently that they had contact with, or were even inspired by other parties, particularly not the Danish or Norwegian Progress Parties. Granted, it is not rare for (radical) right-wing populist parties to deny links with similar parties in an attempt to avoid guilt by association and to thereby limit the risk of their being perceived as excessively nondemocratic or politically extreme. Ian Wachtmeister even avowed explicitly that he had renounced any collaboration with the Danish and Norwegian Progress Parties in order not to be held responsible for their mistakes (Gardberg 1993: 43). The indications are that there was no such collaboration, although there are discernible traces of influence from Glistrup/Kjærsgaard and Carl I. Hagen (the leaders, respectively, of the Danish and Norwegian Progress Parties) in New Democracy's ideological/rhetorical profile, in terms of both style and political content (especially the xenophobic rhetoric).

We might also assume that New Democracy's political entrepreneurs learned several important lessons from the success of the Swedish Green Party in the 1988 election campaign. More specifically, the Green Party showed how far a party can come, and how much media attention it can attract, by adopting a political style at variance with the relative stylistic conformity typical of Swedish politics. New Democracy also appropriated some of the rhetoric that the Greens used in the campaign to the 1988 general election. Both parties, for example, said that they would be a "blowtorch" to the backside of those entrenched in established bureaucratic political procedures. The Green Party promised to bring a direct, more colorful style to politics (see Taggart 1996: 98), and was actually the first to introduce populism and demonstrate its powers.

New Democracy's ideological/rhetorical profile: neoliberalism, xenophobia, and populism

As we have seen, there is some empirical support for the claim that political discontent, the xenophobic niche, and the shift to the right in the socioeconomic cleavage dimension (in descending order) were the primary reasons for the electoral success of New Democracy in 1991. If we look at people's subjective accounts of their choice of party, for instance, we find that no less than 53 percent of those who voted for New Democracy made reference to "fresh new approaches," to the need for "shaking things up," and to the claim that the party "speaks the mind of the common man." Moreover, 19 percent of them referred to the immigration and asylum question, a figure twice that of the other parties. Finally, 11 percent attributed their choice to the party's line on tax, although this was half as many as among Conservative Party supporters (Gilljam & Holmberg 1993: 89–93).

The idea that attitudes pertaining to immigration, political discontent, and neoliberal economic politics were of key importance is further supported by logistic regression analysis. Table 3.2. shows the result from five models, testing the effect of attitudes on the decision to vote for New Democracy.

The first model supports the claim that New Democracy (neither its party ideology nor its electoral base)—contrary to the RRP parties—is not a "culturalistic" party. Authoritarian attitudes, including a strong endorsement of family values and Christian values, and strong antiabortion sentiments were not significantly associated with a higher likelihood to vote for New Democracy.[8] However, congruent with the ideological and rhetorical profile of the party, as will be discussed below, voters preferring stronger punishments and longer terms of imprisonment were three times as likely to vote for New Democracy as voters indifferent to the proposal of implementing such measures.[9]

Table 3.2. Effect of attitudes on the decision to vote for New Democracy in the 1991 election, logistic regression analyses

	Model 1	Model 2	Model 3	Model 4	Model 5
Authoritarianism:					
Family values	0.992				0.945
Christian values	0.984				0.930
Law-and-order (strong)	3.146[3]				2.277
Law-and-order (weak)	2.340[1]				2.201
(Indifferent)	(1.000)				(1.000)
Antiabortion (strong)	0.690				0.734
(Indifferent)	(1.000)				(1.000)
Nationalism/xenophobia:					
Swedish values		1.083			1.115
Too many refugees (strong)		1.841			1.321
(Neither too many nor too few refugees)		(1.000)			(1.000)
Against multiculturalism (strong)		1.534			1.571
(Indifferent)		(1.000)			(1.000)
Reduce aid to developing countries (strong)		2.609[3]			1.350
(Indifferent)		(1.000)			(1.000)
Immigration important issue					2.299[2]
Political discontent:					
Political parties not interested in people's opinions (strongly agree)			3.287[3]		2.653[1]
Political parties not interested in people's opinions (somewhat agree)			2.330[2]		2.161[1]
(Partly disagree)			(1.000)		(1.000)
Very low trust in politicians			3.672[3]		3.238[2]
Rather low trust in politicians			1.630[1]		1.395
(Rather high trust)			(1.000)		(1.000)

(continued)

Table 3.2.—*(continued)*

	Model 1	Model 2	Model 3	Model 4	Model 5
Not at all interested in politics			0.633		0.385
Very interested in politics			1.858[1]		2.089
(Rather interested)			(1.000)		(1.000)
Seldom or never read about politics			1.279		1.349
Voting leads to influence (strongly disagree)			0.641		0.525
(Partly agree)			(1.000)		(1.000)
Very small differences between the parties			2.326[2]		3.411[2]
Rather small differences between the parties			1.612[1]		1.961[2]
(Rather big)			(1.000)		(1.000)
Economic left-right:					
Reduce public sector (strong)				1.497	1.078
(Indifferent)				(1.000)	(1.000)
Strong market economy				1.061	1.136
Less state involvement (strong)				1.909[1]	1.607
(Indifferent)				(1.000)	(1.000)
Inflation priority				0.867	0.887
(Unemployment priority)				(1.000)	(1.000)
Reduce income differences (strongly against)				0.951	0.802
(Indifferent)				(1.000)	(1.000)
Pseudo-R^2	0.031	0.099	0.081	0.068	0.249
Prob>Chi2	0.000	0.000	0.000	0.000	0.000
Log likelihood	-523.79	-474.14	-488.22	-468.47	-335.76
N	2,214	2,198	2,152	2,045	1,646

[1] *Significant on the 0.05 level.*
[2] *Significant on the 0.01 level.*
[3] *Significant on the 0.001 level.*

The second model reveals that voters in strong agreement with the proposal that the state-sponsored aid to developing countries should be reduced were significantly more likely to vote for New Democracy in the 1991 election.[10] However, neither the variables "too many refugees" and "against multiculturalism" nor strong endorsement of "Swedish values" were significantly associated with odds higher than one.[11] Nevertheless, as is shown in model 5, voters stating that the immigration issue was of great importance for their choice of party were more than twice as likely to vote for New Democracy as other voters (while controlling for a battery of other relevant variables).[12]

The third model strongly supports the hypothesis that political discontent was of key importance for the electoral breakthrough of New Democracy. Voters having low trust in politicians and voters strongly believing that political parties are uninterested in the opinion of the voters (but only in their votes) were more than three times as likely to vote for New Democracy, and voters who perceived only very slight differences between the (established) political parties were more than twice as likely to vote for New Democracy.[13] However, it was not the voters uninterested in politics, but on the contrary those taking a strong interest in politics, who showed a significantly higher likelihood to vote for the party.[14]

The fourth model supports the argument of this chapter that New Democracy benefited from a shift to the right within the socioeconomic dimension, by showing that voters strongly preferring less state involvement in the economy were almost twice as likely to vote for the party.[15] Although the other variables failed to show significant associations, the model showed no evidence refuting this argument.

Hence, as we can infer from these results, the best means of exploiting the available opportunity structures was thus to adopt an ideological/rhetorical profile that focused on (1) populist condemnation of the political establishment, (2) anti-immigration sentiments in various forms, and (3) economic neoliberalism.

We shall now therefore turn our attention to the populist antiestablishment strategy, New Democracy's neoliberalism, and its way of appealing to anti-immigration and anti-immigrant opinion.

Neoliberalism

Unlike the RRP parties, New Democracy was essentially an *economistic* party and saw economy and material values as superior to cultural values. This came across particularly strongly in an interview with Bert Karlsson in 1992, in which he asserted that "The economy rules everything. The economy decides everything. . . . Make sure that the economy works in the country, and that country will always be strong" (Gardberg 1993: 80). Neoliberal elements also surfaced in several of the other interviews that Gardberg conducted with a number of New Democracy representatives in the spring of 1992. Johan Brohult MP, for instance, argued that the Liberal Party (which embodies a socioliberal ideology), unlike New Democracy (which, he said, fully embraces free trade and unrestricted competition), is not a liberal party: "We adhere to the father of national economy, Adam Smith, who published a thesis on this 200 years ago" (Gardberg 1993: 80). At the same time, the party took a firm stance on security and law and order, which can be seen as the advocacy of a classic liberal "minimal state," in which public resources are to be channeled into maintaining order and where internal and external security are paramount.

It should also be noted that neoconservative currents, which were otherwise so salient in the policies of Reagan, Thatcher, and the like, were greatly downplayed in New Democracy's political message. Even though these values echoed through the party's "lack of normative standards" (and the links to crime) discourse, through its calls for tougher penalties, and (at least among certain party members) through the necessity of strengthening the (nuclear) family in society (see Gardberg 1993: 84, 89), it was, to repeat, the economy, not sociocultural values, that formed the party's central tenet. Furthermore, no reference was ever made to the importance of "roots," decadence, or the presence of "natural laws" (other than the economic), which is often the case with contemporary RRP parties, in particular those that have a background in the extraparliamentary far right.

Unmistakable elements of a neoliberal ideology can also be read in New Democracy's party manifesto; its 1991 program, for instance, emanated from *The New Welfare* foundation, which was partly funded by the Swedish Employer's Confederation and which oversaw a series of *Citizens' Official Reports* (MOU), a popular source of references for New Democracy. The introductory paragraph of the party manifesto asserted that its policies were and would always be shaped by common sense, personal liberty, and consideration for others. Notable among the manifesto items of relevance here is the demand for a greatly reduced tax burden, which it wanted to see brought to the levels of comparable countries so that people could afford to live on their income. As regards the impact of taxation at an individual level, the party wrote that a greatly reduced tax pressure not only would help motivate working people, it also was a necessary condition of autonomy and personal freedom (Ny demokrati 1991: 4). As for the effects on business and industry, such a move was fundamental to Sweden's economic growth. If Sweden was to stem the flow of investment out of the country and enable companies to expand within its borders, it needed to offer some sort of tax incentive to industry. To finance these tax relief measures, New Democracy wanted to see the sale or privatization of state-run companies and property. This would, moreover, have an intrinsic value as the public sector, they reasoned, had to be reduced, deregulated, and streamlined (Ny demokrati 1991: 4). To this end, they wanted to see the abolition of the monopoly held by hospitals and other health-care institutions, and the national health service complemented with private alternatives—all of which would help to shorten waiting times for operations and other treatments (Ny demokrati 1991: 10f). In a similar vein, New Democracy's manifesto also called for a wider selection of independent schools. Greater choice for pupils and parents was another party goal, as was autonomy for schools, by which their curricula and budgets would be brought under the control of the school management (Ny demokrati 1991: 13).

As we have seen, New Democracy managed to establish itself despite the fact that the Conservative Party was still seen as a right-wing party. In one way, then, the emergence of New Democracy can be considered the product of a process of "outbidding": when the economic winds were blowing strongest from the right, fanned by SAF and Timbro, the Conservative Party was prevented from adopting an overly radical stance (on account of how their policies had to be fairly realistic and implementable should the party end up in power, and of how the party had to be able to align its policies with those of the other prospective coalition parties), leaving New Democracy in a position to up the ante; when the Conservative Party promised tax cuts of 10 billion kronor per year up until the mid 1990s, New Democracy promised tax cuts of 200 billion kronor over the course of six years (see Ungeson 1992: 32f). Both parties also promised that the cuts would be partly funded by "dynamic effects," although the Conservative Party was far more cautious in their estimate of how great these effects would actually be.

Condemning immigration policy: welfare chauvinism and xenophobic ethnopluralism

Four separate themes (or *frames*) can be identified in the (radical) right-wing parties' anti-immigration and anti-immigrant discourse: (1) immigrants are a threat to the Swedish identity and to Swedish culture and values; (2) immigration leads to rising crime, which carries the implication that immigrants are not law-abiding; (3) immigrants put a strain on resources and live on subsidies, which means that immigration drains money from the state coffers, money that otherwise could have gone toward better welfare for "Swedes" or tax cuts; and (4) immigrants take "our" (i.e., "Swedes'") jobs (Rydgren 2003b). While the first two of these frames can be treated as a manifestation of the ethnopluralist doctrine—i.e., that different ethnicities should not "mix" lest cultural specificities should disappear and insecurity and crime increase—the last two can be treated as part of the welfare chauvinist doctrine, in which immigrants and "Swedes" are depicted as competing for limited economic resources. In such a conflict situation, immigrants are portrayed as illegitimate competitors, pitted against Swedes who are *entitled* to keep the entire cake for themselves. This is a zero-sum game in which one side always loses what the other side gains; and the idea that immigration can also produce dynamic effects that help the cake grow for everyone is dismissed as a possibility from the discourse.

New Democracy's anti-immigration and anti-immigrant political message was largely writ in economic terms, sometimes in harmony with the welfare chauvinist doctrine, but most commonly by juxtaposing the costs of immigration with tax cuts. In that Sweden was in a boom period when the party emerged, the job-competition theme was not deployed very often. Nevertheless, examples of the ethnopluralist doctrine can also be identified prior to the election, even if the theme was heavily downplayed in comparison with RRP parties like the Sweden Democrats, the Danish People's Party, or the Front National, and these examples were to grow stronger during 1992 and 1993 (which, of course, cannot be held up as a reason for the party's rise).

Welfare chauvinism

The critical line that New Democracy took regarding immigrants and immigration was very much dressed up in economic terms, as illustrated by this extract from one of Ian Wachtmeister's books: "Why should it be taboo to criticise Swedish asylum and overseas aid policy? For it has not proved at all successful, unless by success one means sending 14,500 million kronor a year to foreign countries and receiving the maximum number of economic refugees into Sweden" (Wachtmeister 1992: 54). In concrete terms, New Democracy's manifesto called for the introduction of temporary residence permits and demanded the immediate assimilation into Swedish society of all those allowed to stay. The party also considered it urgent for immigrants to be put into employment as quickly as possible and for refugees to be granted loans for as long as they were unable to support themselves in Sweden; for as far as New Democracy was concerned, it paid refugees to live on benefits rather than work. Another recurrent theme in their manifesto, and one that reflects the party's insistence on the assimilation of immigrants, was the abolition of "mother tongue teaching," which it considered an unnecessary cost. New Democracy was more critical of refugees than it was of immigrants "who have a job sorted before they arrive," and even within this former group distinguished between political refugees (who were tolerated) and economic refugees (who the party claimed constituted the vast majority of asylum seekers). New Democracy's opposition to such refugees was couched mainly in economic terms as a waste of resources (see Gardberg 1993), the party even going as far as to demand in one campaign leaflet an end to *all* immigration of what it called economic refugees: "Our generous immigration policy has taken in many who not really need to come here," they wrote, while "at the same time we have deported real refugees" (Westlind 1996: 151). As Westlind observes, no explanation was ever given as to what would constitute a "genuine cause," and the party offered no example of the kind of refugee it would welcome.

As part of its welfare chauvinist rhetoric, New Democracy also often pitted immigrants and development aid against pensioners and the care of "our own": "In order for the people of Sweden to support generous aid programs with a clear conscience we must first be convinced that care and nursing is satisfactorily arranged for those that once built up Sweden" (Westlind 1996: 151). Bert Karlsson appealed to Swedish pensioners in a similar manner: "I say to these pensioners, who feel restless because nothing happens, that I of course think it is wrong that one has to seek political asylum in order to make a decent living in Sweden. But I really think that it will soon be the only way!" (Westlind 1996: 151). In a similar vein, an election leaflet from 1991 asked, "Do refugees really have to be better off than the pensioners who worked for their country all their lives?" (Westlind 1996: 152); and the message was repeated yet again in 1992 during New Democracy's reprised electioneering campaign from the summer before, when Bert Karlsson explained to audiences that Swedish asylum policy erodes the care the country can provide for the elderly and handicapped.

The ethnopluralist doctrine

Despite the relatively downplayed presence of the ethnopluralist doctrine in New Democracy's anti-immigrant rhetoric compared to the RRP parties (and this applies to culture and values in general), there were traces of it in the party's political message. In a televised interview in the summer of 1991, for example, Ian Wachtmeister accused African refugees of having introduced the AIDS virus into Sweden, and reeled off cases in which African men had infected Swedish women (Westlind 1996: 149). When considering such accusations, we should not forget that the party had previously called for the AIDS testing of all immigrants, a demand that although deleted from the 1991 manifesto was reinstated when New Democracy tightened up its asylum policy program in November 1993 (Carlberg 1991). Such association of immigrants with disease is a common rhetorical strategy for modern RRP parties, as it was for older far-right parties and movements (see Rydgren 2003b). Later in the interview, Wachtmeister expressed his displeasure at the way Sweden had fewer "ethnic citizens" than other Western European countries, "ethnic citizens" being defined as Swedes of pure or at least two generations' Swedish descent (Westlind 1996: 149). Such fears of "Swedishness" being under attack from an outside world forcing itself over the national boundaries are reminiscent of the rhetoric applied by the French Front National and other RRP parties, and are suggestive of an ethnic nationalist, ethnopluralist canon. This was also touched on by New Democracy MP John Bouvin, who contended that there are just two major problems facing the world: language and religion. "We in the West, we are like a family, we have about the same values," he argued. "It's a question of values" (Gardberg 1993: 101). Bouvin also submitted a parliamentary bill shortly after the 1991 election in which he called for an end to all refugee immigration, justifying his demand by announcing that "we have to solve our own problems first."

This type of rhetoric, which attempted to articulate xenophobia by depicting immigrants as frightening, threatening, and culturally disparate, escalated during the party's term in the Riksdag. During New Democracy's summer campaign of 1993, for example, Vivianne Franzén (who was appointed party leader the following year) described the murder committed by a mentally ill immigrant on his son as a Muslim ritual murder, and on another occasion warned that Swedish school-children would soon have to turn toward Mecca (Granath 1993), rhetoric that seems lifted almost word for word from the manifestos of Le Pen's Front National or Pia Kjærsgaard's Danish People's Party.

To a certain extent, then, there were also elements of the New Democracy rhetoric that attempted to link immigration and crime; indeed, even in its very first manifesto the party had advocated the deportation of refugees who commit serious crimes in Sweden (Ny demokrati 1991: 7)—although John Bouvin for his part argued that shoplifting would constitute adequate grounds for expulsion (Gardberg 1993: 48).

A "soft" xenophobia?

Like the RRP parties, New Democracy wished to conduct a referendum on development aid policy, even if the party contrary to continental RRP parties was not making any direct calls for referenda on immigration and asylum (except for Sten Söderberg MP, who argued for such a measure; see Westlind 1996: 150; Gardberg 1993). We can see this as an expression of the populist antiestablishment strategy: implicit in the demand for referenda is an accusation that the mainstream parties are being "undemocratic" in not allowing the people to have their say in political decisions of this nature. The political establishment was also accused of having deliberately veiled the total cost of immigration behind budget headings such as "social aid" and "correctional treatment."

At the same time, the party's consciously low profile on immigration and asylum referenda might have stemmed from its fear of ending up too far out on the radical flank, with stigmatization the inevitable outcome. Indeed, the party was generally careful in the 1991 election campaign to couch its anti-immigration rhetoric in terms that would have the power to mobilize anti-immigrant—and xenophobic—currents of opinion without its being branded racist. For example, throughout 1991 New Democracy tried to stress that it was not opposed to helping political refugees (which would have come across as inhuman), it just believed that the best way to help them was not to let them enter Sweden. In its leaflet headed "Why are they telling lies about New Democracy?" the party writes, for example, that "If we really want to help many people we have to do it in the area where catastrophes happen. We can't help Somalis by bringing them here. Or?" (Westlind 1996: 146). In a similar vein, New Democracy's proposals that SIDA (the Swedish International Development Cooperation Agency) be abolished and development aid be greatly reduced were justified with the argument that more resources could then be concentrated on the Baltic States, which was where development aid should primarily be channeled (Ny demokrati 1991: 7; see also Westlind 1996: 147). Yet again, the militant John Bouvin MP stepped beyond the pale of this "soft" rhetorical strategy. In explaining why the main recipients of such aid should be the Baltic rather than the African states, he made the following comments: "We must help the Balts, not simply toss lots of misguided projects here and there around Africa. I've seen the effects. In the old days, they would give birth to 15 kids—the lion would eat a couple and ten would die of starvation, leaving three that would survive. Now, with the help of our money, they all survive and we are heading for disaster" (Ungeson 1992: 45). What is interesting is that notwithstanding the reproachful comments of the rest of the parliamentary group, Bouvin was never expelled from the party. The fact is that in his book *The Crocodiles* from 1992, Ian Wachtmeister actually defended Bouvin:

> "You cannot go around saying that African children die of starvation and disease or are even eaten by wild animals. That is obvious. After all, in Swedish minds, Africa is full of starving children who receive help from SIDA [the Swedish International Development Authority] and all the good people from the Arctic circle. Well, is not that the case? And what does Bouvin know? He has only worked as an excavator operator in three developing countries. How can he know what is said amongst the peoples of Africa? He who has got many black friends. Jet black, he says. No, the only ones with any knowledge of Africa [is] SIDA." (Wachtmeister 1992: 50f.)

Here again we have an example of Wachtmeister trying to employ the populist antiestablishment strategy by implying that the voice of "the common man," represented by Bouvin, is being suppressed by the political establishment. Nevertheless, both Bouvin and his apologist stepped over the mark of what is considered extreme in Swedish political culture (by most voters too), and so these comments probably did more harm than good for the party's ability to mobilize voters. As also shown above, less "soft" anti-immigrant/xenophobic remarks as these also became increasingly common during the party's parliamentary term: when repeating its campaign from the summer of 1991, Bert Karlsson in 1992 declared that the so-called "laser man"—who during 1991 spread fear by shooting at "immigrant looking" people; eleven were hit and one died—whose true identity was unknown at the time, was probably both a Liberal and a foreigner, Wachtmeister, for his part, announced that immigrant children travel by limousine to their "mother tongue teaching" classes (Kratz 1992b; Sourander 1992).

Even when looking more into detail of New Democracy's anti-immigrant rhetoric, we find strategies commonly employed by RRP parties like the Sweden Democrats or the French Front National (see Rydgren 2003b; 2004a). One such is to take key concepts and ideas endorsed by political opponents and distort their original meaning by turning the logic on its head, a rhetorical method usually referred to as "frame transformation" (see, e.g., Snow et al 1986; Benford & Snow 2000). This could involve, for instance, focusing on "inverted racism" or "reverse discrimination." In this spirit, New Democracy motioned for legislation to protect young Swedes from being *discriminated against* as a result of the "positive discrimination" of refugees and immigrants. Young Swedes, they argued, should have the same rights and opportunities in society as immigrants, and should not have to be subjected to discrimination at school, at work, or on the housing market (Arter 1992: 367; Gardberg

1993: 48). In arguing thus, the party was implying that "anti-Swedish" racism and discrimination were a more serious problem than xenophobia and discrimination, which *de facto* affected immigrants and other ethnic minorities (see Rydgren 2004c), who were not the targets of their proposed discrimination protection.

Opposed to all elephants and crocodiles: the populist antiestablishment strategy

The foremost method for exploiting the distrust felt for the mainstream parties—and politicians—that had begun to surface among the electorate was to place their own party in sharp contrast to the establishment they were challenging. New Democracy's political rhetoric was thus based on a simple dichotomy of "us versus the rest," all of which were lumped together without acknowledgment of the major differences that existed between them. Whereas New Democracy claimed to represent the common man and common sense, the other parties represented the face of bureaucracy and political elitism and were alienated from the people. This opened the way for a new champion to defend the man in the street, the very person the party claimed to represent. Unlike the mainstream parties, which simply tussled with other individual parties or one of the two political blocs, New Democracy's rhetoric was a challenge to the entire party system. Its message was also based on political simplifications: politics need not be abstruse; all that is needed is a bit of common sense and an ear for what the people want, they reasoned, reducing complex economic reasoning to numbers of beer crates. Apparently, the only obstacle to finding political solutions, the party argued, was the stubborn refusal of the mainstream parties to relinquish political prestige.

Satire was also an important feature of New Democracy's popular appeal: Swedish politics was likened to a duck pond (Wachtmeister 1988) and politicians to elephants, overweight from too much sitting (Wachtmeister 1990), or to crocodiles, with their tiny ears and gaping jaws (Wachtmeister 1992). A typical feature of New Democracy's special populist style was the program item "a better life—more fun and more money in your pocket," which was written into the 1991 manifesto to present a number of ideas they had on how to make life in Sweden more enjoyable, such as the removal of unnecessary prohibitions and the cutting of tax, the distribution of which should be decided by the citizens themselves (Ny demokrati 1991: 14). This represented a merging of the party's populist and neoliberal strains, which were thus rendered virtually indistinguishable.

Certain aspects of New Democracy's neoliberal message can *also* be considered part of the populist antiestablishment strategy, in that the party associated the establishment with a unanimous commitment to a Social Democratic or socioliberal welfare state that demanded a relatively high tax burden. The populist strains in New Democracy's neoliberalism are particularly salient when we consider the spending areas that the party targeted for savings, namely the national, regional, and local government bureaucracy (considered part of the political establishment). Bert Karlsson, for example, advocated the abolition of "public funding for organizations in Sweden, that are part of the political establishment . . . public funding for parties, the press . . . There is also the waste of money at the immigration office . . ." (quoted in Gardberg 1993: 80). Another example of this is New Democracy's alcohol policy, which was a high-profile issue for the party during the election campaign. In an effort to bring bar prices in line with those of the state-run Systembolag off-licenses, the party demanded that restaurants and pubs be granted the same trade discount for beer, wine, and spirits as that applied to other commodities; it also advocated the sale of beer and wine in supermarkets, as was the case in the rest of the EC. In laying out such demands, New Democracy wanted to promote a culture in which drinking was an accepted and integral part, since it was convinced that the main problem with the country's alcohol policy was that people simply could not afford to socialize. After all, families in other countries could manage to visit a restaurant at least once a month, why not in Sweden? And it was here that the roots of many people's loneliness lay (Ny demokrati 1991: 15). Swedish alcohol policy was an apposite issue to target in their populist critique of bureaucracy and government control; indeed the leader of the populist Skåne Party, Carl Herslow, had already demonstrated the potential for popular support inherent to challenging the country's restrictive line on alcohol by using the very same strategy back in the mid 1980s (Peterson et al. 1989). In a similar vein, New Democracy lobbied for the abolition of traffic wardens.

There can be no doubt, therefore, that New Democracy did everything in its power to use the first component of the populist antiestablishment strategy by profiling itself as an alternative to the entire "political class." It also resolved in its manifesto to amend the constitution on a number of points, demanding the introduction of a more candidate-based election system to increase citizen influence and raise the credibility capital of the country's politicians; it also called for the greater use of referenda for the same reasons (Ny demokrati 1991: 3). There are, however, even more explicit expressions of the first component of the antiestablishment strategy in the interviews Gardberg (1993) conducted with leading party members: according to Johan Brohult, for instance, New Democracy was opposed to corruption and political power. "We want the citizens to have the power," he said. "We don't believe in representative democracy in the manner it exists now, where trade union bosses represent the workers and the big elephants in parliament and government represent the citizens" (Gardberg 1993: 90). One campaign slogan during the summer of 1991 was "Power to the People, not to the iron-butts," the latter being the nickname they gave to the bureaucrats whom the party accused of sitting too comfortably and for too long on their backsides (Westlind 1996: 135). According to party member Harriet Colliander, Ny demokrati listened to the "common man," and sought to solve political problems using nothing but common sense (Gardberg 1993: 90). Bert Karlsson also claimed that the party represented the "will of the people": "If people are strange, we are strange as well," he said, "because I think we say how people want it" (Gardberg 1993: 90). On the whole, New Democracy did not shy away from the term *populism*; indeed, they even tried to turn the epithet into something positive. Take this extract from Ian Wachtmeister's book *The Crocodiles* for example: "If populism is about talking in a way that people understand, then I hope that Bert and I will remain populists until our dying days. The thing about politicians is that they talk in a way that goes over people's heads. Often even over the head of a professor of linguistics" (Wachtmeister 1992: 91). All in all, then, New Democracy's political rhetoric may serve as a textbook example of the populist antiestablishment strategy as presented in chapter 1.

New Democracy also employed a political style that harbored a lack of respect for democratic political institutions and procedures. For example, Bert Karlsson compared parliamentary ballots with the Eurovision Song Contest in which he was involved (Widfeldt 2004) and was photographed by the tabloid paper *Expressen* standing in his stockinged feet on the debating chamber's rostrum during the general election of 1991. Other strategies were used to reinforce the party's folksy, common image and to attract the attention of the media as well as the voters, such as taking part in the popular celebrity soccer matches (in which Karlsson played and which Wachtmeister occasionally refereed) during the election campaign of 1991. As Karlsson wrote with reference to an election meeting in Grebbestad in early July that year: "I played soccer with the TV celebrity team. Ian was ref. A huge crowd turned up to watch. We combined several appearances that summer with the TV team. Bengt Bedrup [a television journalist] gave us a lot of publicity" (Karlsson 1991: 78f).

Like most other (radical) right-wing populist parties, New Democracy was reluctant to position itself on the right-left political scale. The party's representatives either contended that it was positioned somewhere in the middle or denied the value of such a scale in the first place. As Johan Brohult MP declared: "We don't think you should have a right-left scale. It counteracts its own aims. Our opponents place us at the very right edge because they don't want to deal with us" (Gardberg 199: 88).

Even though New Democracy, in line with the populist antiestablishment strategy, did all it could to not appear antidemocratic, it still claimed that contemporary Swedish democracy was rotten to the core, paralyzed by a political establishment and a union movement predisposed to settling matters *in camera*. These were the "elephants" in Wachtmeister's words (Gardberg 1993: 47). Notwithstanding all efforts to appear democratic and as the "champions of true democracy," leading party members still let slip remarks that hinted at a much greater disrespect for democracy as a political system. According to Karlsson, for instance, it "doesn't matter how things look before you reach a decision" as long as the decision is a sound one and of benefit to the people. "If it is undemocratic or what the heck, I wouldn't give a damn, as long as the decision is fair" (quoted in Gardberg 1993: 107). Karlsson went on to state in an interview in the men's magazine *Café* in the winter of 1991 that one party and one leader is all a country really needs, for otherwise there is too much squabbling (Ungeson 1992: 27). And going one step further, John Bouvin even proclaimed that "a little dictatorship is good for the people," reinforcing this creed with an exhortation to the Riksdag to "go to hell." As mentioned before, Bouvin was never expelled for such remarks, and he continued to assert that Sweden was not a democracy: Our politicians "just sit here, a little bunch, and decide what we shall do" (Gardberg 1993: 107).

To the extent that these and similar pronouncements damaged the party, New Democracy was always able to bounce back. In other contexts too, the party managed to turn blunders to their strategic benefit. A typical example of this is Karlsson's appearance on the television show *Magasinet* on 15 February 1991, when the party was still in its infancy. As mentioned above, the show's host Olle Stenholm plied him with a series of tricky but relevant questions about New Democracy's political line, questions to which Karlsson was unable to supply any answers. In response to this and the ensuing media storm, Karlsson decided to step down as party leader. Subsequently, the party skillfully exploited his failure by portraying it as an example of the establishment's supercilious attitude toward common people. Karlsson accused the establishment of having "ganged up on New Democracy" and raged in indignation over the way he and his party were treated (Ungeson 1992: 17). When he returned as party leader a mere six days after his resignation, Karlsson justified his decision in *Expressen* thus: "I can't quit just like that . . . I'd be a fool not to listen to what the people wanted . . . Priests are praying for me in churches. People are calling me up, begging me to stay on as party leader" (Ungeson 1992: 17). Yet again, and in this new way, New Democracy was painting a picture of conflict between the Establishment and the People, on whose behalf Ny demokrati and Bert Karlsson took up arms. After these events, everyone expected New Democracy to plummet in the polls; but it was not to be, and the party increased its share to 11.8 percent in Domoskop's subsequent survey. The fact that the party sustained no damage was further confirmed by Sifo's poll of 28 April, which gauged the party's support at 9.1 percent (Rydgren 1996).

This suggests that media exposure per se is so powerful that it is able to offset adverse publicity. We could also venture that such events actually benefit emerging right-wing populist parties as they facilitate the use of the antiestablishment strategy. There are even more signs that "negative" media publicity was considered a succor to New Democracy, at least that is before its internal conflicts began to do it serious harm. Their greatest fear was ending up in the media shadow, as the party lacked alternative campaign strategies. Karlsson later admitted that he had not "done his homework" when he took part in Olle Stenholm's *Magasinet* (Karlsson 1991: 52) and that he had used the occasion to attract media attention:

> The truth is that I had constantly refused to be party leader, but Ian persuaded me. We had been a little unsure about who was to do what in the party and how people would react to Ian being in the executive. Whatever, I wanted to step down anyway, and it had nothing to do with Olle Stenholm. In my mind, Ian would have made a better leader. The reason why I announced my resignation during [the popular radio program] *After three* was that I wanted to exploit the occasion. I gambled, to be frank, and exploited the fact that I had made a fool of myself. I realized that people would sympathies with me, that they would relate to the situation. *Magasinet* became a symbol of attitudes towards common people: whoever has not studied politics full time or who does not understand the ins and outs of economics after just a fortnight has not got a hope (Karlsson 1991: 58f).

New Democracy's party organization: *business,* but not *as usual*

So far, we have seen how the rise of New Democracy coincided with opportunity structures that favored a political message that combined neoliberalism, (xenophobic) anti-immigrant sentiments and a populist critique of the political establishment. We have also seen how New Democracy presented such an explicit message. What remains for us to discuss is New Democracy's organizational structure and its ability to mobilize resources. As might be recalled from chapter 2, we may assume that (A) newly formed parties lacking a party history are at an advantage on the voter arena, as the potential conflict between the internal arena and the voter arena is less salient, particularly if they have (B) a hierarchical or even authoritarian party structure and (C) access to external resources (i.e., money and/or media), which reduces the reliance on party members. New Democracy fitted this description perfectly. It was not only newly formed and therefore without a party history (with which party members could identify), but also extremely hierarchical in its power structure. Even though the party's own statistics gave it a membership of 5,000 in 1991, roughly the same as the Green Party at the time (Widfeldt 1997: 266f), none but a select elite had any real opportunity to influence decisions.

Unlike the other Swedish parties, New Democracy had no regional organization. Although the party professed to having a flat organizational structure (see Taggart 1996: 122f) by pointing to the opportunities that existed for direct contact between the local councils and the national party executive, it was in fact very much controlled from the top down, even from its very inception. Looking at it another way, we can interpret the lack of regional associations as simply a way of saving money and of giving the leadership more room for maneuver. In fact, there were never any real attempts by the party leadership to build up a nationwide network of local organizations. Such bodies did spring up spontaneously in 1991 as the party started to draw more and more attention, but they operated without any financial support from the party executive (to cover the costs of printing ballot papers, etc.), in spite of their resolve to stand in the local council elections under the party's banner; instead, they were charged 2,000 kronor for the license to use the party's name and logo (Westlind 1996: 158f). The party leadership also opposed the initiatives taken by the local associations to establish a coherent, nationwide party organization (Westlind 1996: 159). As we will be discussing further in the next chapter, instead of having any kind of local organizational level, after 1993 New Democracy adopted a system of contracts that it required independent local parties to sign before they could use the name New Democracy (Widfeldt 1997: 38). And unlike all other Riksdag parties, New Democracy had neither a women's organization nor a youth league (Widfeldt 1997: 83). In other words, it is clear that New Democracy had no interest at all in establishing a "social movement." Although this no doubt benefited the party in the short term, it served only to hasten its rapid dissipation just a few years later (as we will see in the next chapter).

A further illustration of the party's authoritarian control can be found in the way its election candidates were not nominated by members around the country (as is normally the case for other parties) but handpicked by its two party leaders. Wachtmeister was particularly keen to recruit candidates from his circle of friends and acquaintances, although some of those who had spontaneously contacted the party immediately after its founding also ended up on the ballot slips. It was Wachtmeister who composed the party manifesto and he who controlled its official policies (Taggart 1996: 125f). Yet in spite of this (as we discussed above, and as will become even clearer in the following chapter) he was not always able to enforce the control over the party group and individual party members.

The likely goals of New Democracy's organizational form were not only to maximize its effectiveness but also to disassociate it from other parties (in line with the populist antiestablishment strategy). By tradition, Swedish politics is intentionally deliberative and "participant intensive," and pressure groups have always been given ample room for maneuver in practical political space (Widfeldt 2004). However, this involved a degree of inertia, and perhaps created the impression that the inertia was greater than it actually was. Such inaction was anathema to New Democracy, who pledged to bring efficiency to the political process—to make it, as they said, more "businesslike" (Widfeldt 2004). There was thus a conscious decision to organize the party along the lines of a listed company, a structural form that is almost by definition nondemocratic in nature (see, e.g., Schattschneider 1975; Pierre 1999).

New Democracy also managed to acquire considerable elbow room on the voter arena by virtue of its ability to find alternative resources for electoral mobilization. As a newly formed party, New Democracy was excluded from the Government party subsidy program, the principal source of income for all mainstream parties (Pierre & Widfeldt 1994: 348). Such disentitlement makes it extremely difficult for many other unestablished parties to finance, say, the printing of ballot papers and the general campaign material necessary for them to broadcast their message. Despite this, New Democracy was able to acquire much of the resources it needed through its contacts with the corporate world and the generous free publicity offered by the media (see Gardberg 1993: 51). New Democracy was a typical media party. It exploited the media's craving for the unexpected and the spectacular, and in so doing rendered it less reliant on labor-intensive resources;

but, as we shall see later, this also left it more vulnerable to media exclusion and neglect.

One should exercise caution when talking of charisma, which is one of the most abused terms in all political analysis. Nevertheless we would not be reckless in maintaining that New Democracy fulfilled several of the criteria identified by Panebianco (1988: 145ff) as characteristic of a *charismatic party*: (1) the party must have been formed by the party leader to realize his or her personal goals; (2) the party leader must be alone in choosing those with whom he or she is to work; (3) the party leader must be the sole (or at least the main) interpreter of the party's political doctrine, which (4) creates an organization comprising a dominant group united by a strength of loyalty to the leader (which counters factionalism as long as the leader is seen as authoritative); (5) internal career paths must be closed to those not favored by the party leader, partly as a result of elite recruitment and partly (6) through the imposition of a high degree of centralization; and (7) the party must usually be an antiparty party that presents itself as an alternative to all others (cf. Weber 1978). However, New Democracy's problem ultimately lay in there being two party leaders (even though Wachtmeister was the real leader, Karlsson was considered a leader by some of the party activists). This triggered early discord, although splits did not appear until after the 1991 general election. So as much as this organizational form helped the rise of New Democracy in the short term, it also eventually proved a severe obstacle to its survival.

In conclusion, we can say that New Democracy's organization was well adapted to exploiting the niches that had opened up on the voter arena. Because the party was newly formed and without any party history, and because of the party executive's iron hold on the members (few Swedish parties have been as authoritarian as New Democracy), it managed to avoid many of the limitations that normal parties have to contend with. It generally takes a long time for parties to have decisions on policy reform accepted and approved, as party members and activists often identify themselves with the traditional party line, and so there is always a latent conflict between the voter and party arenas (see chapter 2). However, New Democracy emerged largely unscathed from such conflict in the run-up to the 1991 election, and found itself with the balance of power in its hands—a strategy decision that is not so easy for other parties to make by virtue of their traditional and/or emotional allegiance to either one of the political groupings or blocs. I would therefore like to contend that New Democracy's poorly developed organization was an advantage to the party for the election of 1991. However, as we shall soon see, it eventually proved the main instrument of the party's disintegration.

Notes

1. See Gummesson (1992) for a discussion about how the plans to form a party may have been hatched well before this time.

2. For readers who are unfamiliar with logistic regressions, Table 3.1 should be read in the following way: Instead of displaying coefficients (b), as is common in OLS regressions, odds ratios (e^b) are used. The odds ratio shows how the odds of the "event" are influenced by changes in the independent variables. It is defined as [odds (if the independent variable is increased by 1) / odds (if the variable is not incremented)]. The odds, in turn, are defined as P / (1-P) where P is the probability of the event. For example, an odds ratio of 2 means that the odds of the event are doubled by a one-unit increase in the independent variable. A value of 1 means that the change in the independent variable has no effect on the odds, and an odds ratio of 0.5 means that the odds of the event halve as the independent variable increases by 1. Odds ratios greater than 1 thus signify positive relationships, odds ratios less than 1 negative relationships, and odds ratios equal to 1 no relationship at all. Log likelihood is a value for the overall fit of the model, whereas pseudo-R^2 provides a way to describe or compare the fit of different models for the same dependent variable (cf. Hamilton 1998: 225–249; Pampel 2000).

3. In analyzing the sociological and demographic basis of New Democracy's voters (and later their attitudes) I use data from the "Swedish Election Survey" 1991 (SSD 0391) primarily collected by Michael Gilljam and Sören Holmberg at Gothenburg University. The sample size of the survey was 3,700 Swedish voters (aged between 18 and 80), 970 voters chose not to participate, leaving the size of the net sample 2,730 persons. 169 respondents reported that they had voted for New Democracy in the election. The variables measuring professions are dummies that correspond to categories in the questionnaire. I have used "Employees/officials" as reference category.

4. The variables "low education" and "university level education" are dummies. The former was constructed by adding together the answers "elementary school" and "nine-year compulsory school" to the question of what was the highest level of education the IP had reached. The latter correspond to a category in the questionnaire. The dummy "more than compulsory school, less than senior high-school" was also included in the model, but not in Table 3.1, and was composed by adding three answers to the same question. The variable "senior high-school" was used as reference category. The variable "unemployed" is also a dummy, corresponding to an actual category in the questionnaire. Six other different terms of employment were included in the model (but not shown in Table 3.1) and the variable "full employed" was used as reference category.

5. The category "impaired personal economy" is a dummy, corresponding the answer "impaired" to the question of how the IP's personal economy had developed during the last few years. Also the variable "improved personal economy" was included in the model (but not in Table 3.1) and the variable "no change in personal economy" was used as reference category.

6. Other events that caused serious problems for the Social Democrats during the latter half of the 1980s include the abolition of credit and currency controls, the tax deal with the Liberal Party, and the abolition of collective affiliation for members in the Swedish Trade Union Confederation to the Social Democratic Party.

7. It should be noted here that this amendment also benefited the Christian Democrats; in fact it was very much due to pressure from this party that the policy was changed in the first place.

8. The variable "anti-abortion, strong" is a dummy, constructed from the original coding that separated between "strongly agree," "somewhat agree," "neither agree nor disagree," "somewhat disagree," and "strongly disagree" as reactions to the proposal that the right of abortion should be limited. All categories, expect the third one, which was used as reference category, were included in the model (although only the first is shown in Table 3.2). The reason for creating dummy variables rather than using the original coding as a continuous variable was twofold: first, the relative distance between the values is uncertain (e.g., is the step from "strongly agree" to "somewhat agree" equally large as the step from "somewhat agree" to "neither agree nor disagree"?); second, one may theoretically assume that voters sharing strong attitudes for or against things are more likely to vote according to their attitudes than voters sharing only lukewarm attitudes. The variable "Christian values" is continuous on a 10-degree scale from 0 (= very bad proposal to promote a society strongly influenced by Christian values) to 10 (= very good proposal). The variable "family values" is coded in the same way (0 = very good proposal to promote a society in which the role of the family is strong; 10 = very bad proposal).

9. The variable "law-and-order" is a dummy constructed from the original coding that separated between "strongly agree," "somewhat agree," "neither agree nor disagree," "somewhat disagree," and "strongly disagree" as reactions to the proposal that criminals should be punished harder. All categories, except the third one—which was used as reference category—were included in the model (although only the first two ones were shown in Table 3.2).

10. The variable "reduce aid to developing countries" is a dummy, constructed from the original coding that separated between "strongly agree," "somewhat agree," "neither agree nor disagree," "somewhat disagree," and "strongly disagree" as reactions to the proposal to reduce financial aid to developing countries. All categories, except the third one—which was used as reference category—were included in the model (although only the first is shown in Table 3.2).

11. The variable "against multiculturalism" is a dummy, constructed from the original coding that separated between "strongly agree," "somewhat agree," "neither agree nor disagree," "somewhat disagree," and "strongly disagree" as reactions to the proposal to increase the financial support to immigrants to make sure that they preserve their own culture. All categories, except the third one—which was used as reference category—were included in the model (although only the first is shown in Table 3.2). The variable "too many refugees" was coded in the same way, although the stated proposal was to permit fewer refugees residence in Sweden. The variable "Swedish values" is continuous and ranges between 0 (= very bad proposal to promote a society defending traditional Swedish values) and 10 (very good proposal).

12. This variable is a dummy, comprising voters who declared that immigration was an important issue for their choice of party. The reference category is those voters who did not say that immigration was important for their decision how to vote.

13. The variable "political parties not interested in people's opinion" is a dummy, constructed by the answers "fully agree," "partly agree," "partly disagree," and "strongly disagree" to the statement that MPs are uninterested in the opinion of

common people. All categories, expect the second one—which was used as reference category—were included in the model (although only the two last ones are shown in Table 3.2). The variable "low trust in politicians" is a dummy, constructed by the answers "very high trust," "rather high trust," "rather low trust," and "very low trust" to the question of their trust in Swedish politicians. All categories, except the second one—which was used as reference category—were included in the model (although only the two last ones are shown in Table 3.2). The variable "small differences between the parties" is a dummy, constructed by the answers "very big differences," "rather big differences," "no significant references," and "very small differences." All categories, except the second one— which was used as reference category—were included in the model (although only the two last ones are shown in Table 3.2).

14. The variable "interested in politics" is a dummy, constructed by the answers "very interested," "rather interested," "not particularly interested," and "not at all interested." All categories, except the second one—which was used as reference category—were included in the model (although only the first and the last are shown in Table 3.2).

15. The variable "less state involvement" is a dummy, constructed from the original coding that separated between "very good proposal," "rather good proposal," "neither good nor bad proposal," "rather bad proposal," and "very bad proposal" to reduce the state's role in the economy. All categories, except the third one—which was used as reference category—were included in the model (although only the first is shown in Table 3.2). The variables "reduce the public sector" and "reduce income differences" are constructed in the same way. The variable "strong market economy" is continuous, and is ranging between 0 (= very bad proposal to promote increased market economy) to 10 (= very good proposal). The variable "inflation priority" is a dummy, comprising voters giving politics fighting rising inflation priority to politics fighting unemployment. The reference category is voters making the opposite priority.

4

THE FALL OF NEW DEMOCRACY

As we shall see below, New Democracy's success was only a short-lived one; the party gradually fell apart during its parliamentary term, eventually vanishing from the Riksdag with a meager 1.2 percent of the vote in the 1994 general election. The first cracks started to show shortly after the 1991 election, and when Ian Wachtmeister resigned as party leader in February 1994, its disintegration was inevitable. Although the main reason for the party's demise was its lack of organizational backbone, the deep recession into which the country had been plunged had also turned public opinion away from New Democracy's political profile. This chapter will be largely devoted to these two particular factors.

A party increasingly out of step

As we saw in the preceding chapter, one of the catalysts behind the growth of the party was the powerful shift to the right in the socioeconomic dimension before the 1991 general election. Gradually, however, this shift slowed down and changed direction to a shift to the left as the economic crisis began to take hold. Already by 1992, the proportion of voters placing themselves on the right on the political spectrum had declined from 37 to 30 percent, whereas the proportion of those considering themselves "left" doubled from 19 to 37 percent between 1990 and 1994 (Weibull & Holmberg 1993: 4; 1994: 5; 1995: 3). A further sign of this general shift to the left is the change in voter attitude toward public sector cuts. While public opposition to such a measure increased from 18 to 43 percent between 1990 and 1993, public support for less welfare state funding dropped from 56 to 32 percent (Nilsson 1994: 71). There was a similar pattern among voters who believed it a very good proposal to reduce the public sector: an increase of 11 to 21 percent for, and a decline from 24 percent to 10 percent against[1] (See Nilsson 1995). As a consequence, support for the Social Democrats soared in the polls, securing the party an impressive 50.4 percent in a Sifo survey in January 1993 (Holmberg 1993: 45f). New Democracy found itself increasingly out of step with the times, and unlike the period in the 1991 general election campaign, its political profile was not very well adapted to the niches and political opportunity structures that presented themselves for the election of 1994.

The economic crisis also contributed to the shrinking size of the anti-immigrant/immigration niche, despite the fact that the immigration and asylum issue was further politicized at the start of the 1990s, partly as a result of New Democracy's political rhetoric. Between 1991 and 1992, the proportion of voters who thought the acceptance of more refugees into Sweden a "poor" or "very poor" proposal increased from 53 to 64 percent (39 percent for the latter) (Demker 1993: 135f). Even though Swedes became more favorably inclined toward asylum seekers and immigrants between 1992 and the 1994 election (Demker 1995: 57), the proportion of anti-immigrant/immigration attitudes remained largely the same then as it was in 1991. It is also worth noting that New Democracy's collapse—rather than its rise—coincided with Sweden's then-largest refugee wave ever (79,000 individuals received residence permits in 1994, most from the former Yugoslavia). We should also bear in mind, however, that the asylum issue, and sociocultural issues in general, became less of a concern to Swedish voters during this time. The economic crisis lifted traditional issues relating to the political economy and the welfare state to a higher level of salience at the expense of issues belonging to the sociocultural dimension (Rydgren 2002, 2003c; Holmberg 2000: 114). A possible reason for this is the way that the new nonsocialist takeover in 1991, which was preceded by an explicit ideological campaign slogan "A new start for Sweden," coincided with the start of the economic crisis. Given that the country was being led for the first time in modern history by a government dominated by the Conservative Party, and that the Government initially attempted to implement its privatization and deregulation policies, it was the left, not least Social Democracy, that became the natural alternative for discontented voters. To go back to chapter 2, we could thus conclude that the economic crisis repoliticized the socioeconomic cleavage dimension and, thus, depoliticized the sociocultural cleavage dimension. This was obviously not advantageous for New Democracy, especially as the political winds had turned to the left, and is a possible reason for the 1994 election fiasco.

New Democracy's problem, as we shall also see below, was that all these changes made it more difficult, if not impossible, for the party to keep its three supporter categories (neoliberals, opponents of immigration/immigrants, and the protest voters/populists) happy all at the same time. This was a historic coalition of voter groups and one that was possible only during the late 1980s and early 1990s. In the mid 1990s, however, a combination of populism, xenophobia, and "left-wing economics" (combined in a protectionist welfare chauvinism) would have been much better suited to mobilize voters. Most RRP parties, led by the Front National, also moved in this direction at this time (Rydgren 2003b). However, as we shall soon see, New Democracy was neither able nor willing to undergo such an ideological and rhetorical change. This made the party even more out of step with the times from the perspective of vote maximization.

Another badly timed strategic error by New Democracy was to persist in its defense of the EU. Opposition to Swedish membership rose sharply from 17 percent to 62 percent from 1990 to 1992 (Lindahl 1993: 154), and even though opinion turned again in the year before the referendum in 1994 (in which 52.2 percent voted for and 46.9 against—see Lindahl 1995: 139), the heavy politicization of the issue presented possibilities for mobilization, arguably for the EU-skeptics most of all. Unlike RRP parties in other countries, New Democracy missed its chance to combine EU opposition with nationalism, xenophobia, and populism, which could have appealed to a relatively large number of anti-EU voters who did not share the other EU-skeptic parties' (the Left, Center, and Green parties) remaining political values (see Rydgren 2002). It should also be noted that New Democracy's party executive also disagreed with their own voters on this issue: in 1993 more New Democracy sympathizers were against Swedish accession to the EU than were for it (40 percent and 31 percent respectively; see Lindahl 1994: 46).

These political developments made it more difficult for New Democracy to win over voters on the ideology they pursued before the 1991 election. In consequence, elements within the party, even within the executive, appealed for urgent changes of direction, and in so doing highlighted the lack of strategies possessed by the party for dealing with internal conflict. And as we shall see, the party's collapse and electoral failure in 1994 all boils down to these organizational factors.

Organizational weaknesses

As we have already noted, New Democracy was formed a matter of
months before the election, leaving it no time to establish an efficient organization. Nor was there any interest in doing so among the leadership:
the party was to be run like a company, with the managing director making the decisions to be then implemented by others under his command.
This proved a recipe of only ephemeral success, for as we discussed in
chapters 2 and 3, newly formed parties can derive short-term strategic
benefit from the way in which the lack of a party history makes it easier
for them to avoid the potential goal conflict that exists between the voter
arena and the internal arena. This is particularly true of the parties with a
strictly hierarchical or even authoritarian party structure as well as access
to external resources (i.e., money and/or the media), which reduces their
dependency on party members. These advantages can, however, turn
against a party in the long run, such as when the new party's membership suddenly increases rapidly as a result of electoral successes, when
its access to external resources decreases, or when there are no internal
tools for handling splits and conflicts within the party organization. RRP
parties winning representation to the political arena can also be hit especially hard by the goal conflicts described in chapter 2 as they are thus
rendered less able to continue using the populist antiestablishment strategy with any real credibility.

Problems on the internal arena

New Democracy's problem in the internal arena was the materialization
of two different disintegration tendencies, one involving a conflict between the party leadership and the members, and one *within* the leadership itself.

The first signs of a split between the leadership and the members appeared relatively soon after the 1991 general election. Even by the general
party conference at the end of February 1992 there was a visible rupture
between the executive and the rest of the organization. One of the principal issues on the party conference agenda was New Democracy's new
organizational charter, and as mentioned earlier, this organization lacked
a formal local county level. The official reason for the proposed reform
was to "bring the leadership closer to the grass roots" (Kratz 1992a);
a more cynical interpretation is that it would increase the executive's
power over the local associations. Indeed, such accusations were leveled
by party executive member Thomas Lindström, who complained that

New Democracy was far too much under the authoritarian control of Ian Wachtmeister and Bert Karlsson (*Folkbladet* 22 Feb 1992). Plans for a reorganization continued to be one of the primary causes of the party's internal quarrels. In 1992, for instance, five New Democracy members were expelled, two of whom were members of the party executive, ostensibly because they actively tried to oppose the implementation of the new order (Knutsson 1992). This first reorganization, however, turned out to be just the beginning. At New Democracy's municipal conference in February 1993, the leadership presented yet another organizational proposal, according to which New Democracy would become a pure national party, with which the local associations would be obliged to sign contracts for the right to use its logo (following the franchise model used by McDonald's and others). Ahead of the general party conference in April that same year, Wachtmeister staked his entire political prestige on the issue of the new organization; Karlsson too threatened to resign if the party conference rejected the proposal (Knutsson 1993). There were, however, many of New Democracy's members, even at higher levels, who were highly critical. One such, Jonas Lind, denounced the new order in a debate article in *Dagens Nyheter* under the title "Wachtmeister's Coup." The proposal, he argued, would place too much power into the hands of the leaders, and would thus undermine the party's internal democracy. Despite such internal criticism, the party conference voted in favor of the new order by a solid margin.

Nonetheless, condemnation of the new organization gradually mounted among the party's local organizations. Twelve districts finally held a protest conference in Jönköping in August of 1993, as a consequence of which three more members were expelled from the party (Ljungberg 1993). The conflict escalated further, culminating in the formation of a municipal association of the oppositional fraction in September 1993. A working group was also formed to contend with Wachtmeister and Karlsson and to have the new organization ultimately declared invalid (Rydgren 1995: 44f).

On the internal arena, New Democracy also had problems with its parliamentary group of MPs, and on 11 March 1992 the party saw its first two defectors. The remark by John Bouvin suggesting that Sweden would benefit from a blend of democracy and dictatorship sparked off a debate in the party chambers about whether or not he should be expelled. In the end he was allowed to keep his seat, but as a result of the internal discussions MPs Lars Andersson and Sten Söderberg, who both supported Bouvin (and who were later accused of trying to infiltrate New Democracy on behalf of the Progress Party), withdrew from the party, claiming to be sick and tired of Wachtmeister's "dictatorial manner" (*Östgöta Correspondenten* 12 March 1992). That December, the party also lost Johan Brohult, who attributed his resignation, which was announced directly from the speaker's rostrum in the debating chamber, to Wachtmeister's attempt to veto the nomination of Christina Rogestam (the former head of the Immigration Board) as president of the universities' real estate company (which he saw as a personal vendetta on Wachtmeister's part). He was joined ten months later by Anne Rehnman, who claimed to be unhappy with the anti-refugee comments made by Vivianne Franzén (see previous chapter) and with Wachtmeister's autocratic posturing.

The New Democracy executive, which was effectively made up of Ian Wachtmeister and Bert Karlsson, tried to hold the Riksdag party together by introducing a series of controversial measures. In response to a number of contentious media statements by ill-informed New Democracy MPs, the party executive decided in November 1992 to grant exclusive rights of comment in the party's name to Karlsson and Wachtmeister and their party secretaries (Ljungaeus 1992). Owing to the rising number of defections and the risk of new ones, the party's various MPs were also forced to sign a contract in March 1993 binding them to quit the Riksdag altogether should they decide to leave New Democracy (Ronge 1993a).

Relations within the inner executive, that is to say between Wachtmeister and Karlsson, also started to show signs of disintegration. In actual fact, it is likely that there was a split between Wachtmeister (and his group of followers) and Karlsson (and his—albeit smaller—group of followers) even from the start, a dissonance probably caused by a combination of factors including not only a power struggle but also, and I would not want to underestimate the importance of this, the different approaches they had to the populist antiestablishment strategy (cf. Taggart 1996: 88). For Wachtmeister, populism was simply a *strategy* toward reaching his realpolitik goals as laid out in the party manifesto (perhaps chiefly the neoliberal economic program, but also immigrant policy). Once the party had seats in the Riksdag, Wachtmeister was prepared to tone down the populist rhetoric in favor of strategies most suited to the game to be played out in the parliamentary arena. As things were, such a strategy could just as much have been negotiation as confrontation. For Karlsson, on the other hand, it seems that the populist strategy was of much more profound personal importance. His main political drive was not one of realpolitik; the struggle against the "political establishment" was, for him, *the* political goal above all others. This leads me to suspect that Karlsson saw populism not just as a strategy for winning seats but as an ideology in itself.

Even as early as the televised economic debate in September 1991 Bert Karlsson was openly critical of Ian Wachtmeister: "Ian no longer talks like common people. My mother-in-law didn't understand a word he said" (Grahnquist 1991)—which implies that according to Karlsson, Wachtmeister was not playing the populist antiestablishment strategy hard enough. Wachtmeister no longer talked like a common person but like a politician, criticism that was directed not at what Wachtmeister said but at how he said it. There were also distinct signs of a split the day after the election, when Karlsson presented a list of demands and ultimatums for the coming government in defiance of Wachtmeister's explicit disapproval (Grahnquist 1991). While Wachtmeister wanted to wait and see if the situation was best suited to cooperation or confrontation, Karlsson had no such qualms. For him, the slogan "putting the pazazz into politics" remained a valid motto also after the party had won representation to the Swedish parliament. The split between the two also manifested itself after the party's agreement with the Government on the use of wage earners' investment funds. Having helped save the Government's face, a delighted Wachtmeister said it was the best agreement the party could obtain; Karlsson, on the other hand, strongly disapproved. "If the bourgeoisie are going to call the shots," he grumbled, "then we are not needed as a party" (Wendel 1992). Even back then, Karlsson was talking about two currents within New Democracy; one (represented by him) that wanted the party to follow its own lead without testing the general political response beforehand, and one that, as far as he was concerned, knew little about taking autonomous, nonpartisan action (*Svenska Dagbladet*, 14 May 1992).

Bert Karlsson had, then, disapproved of Ian Wachtmeister's strategy to maximize the party's implementation potential through compromise. His partner's reluctance to overthrow the nonsocialist Government also grated with him. One of the central themes of the populist antiestablishment strategy is the need for a new political force beyond the established party conflicts; hence Karlsson's reaction to the realization that Wachtmeister had opted to favor the nonsocialist (i.e., bourgeois) camp in Swedish politics. Karlsson would have liked to overthrow the Government to show up the inherent weakness of the political mainstream: "Ian had the opportunity to overthrow the Government using New Democracy's policies in the spring of 1993. The Social Democrats would have then had to have stepped in and put the cards on the table. That would have shown that a Social Democrat government also has to make tough savings and that all their talk of special solidarity with society's most vulnerable is nothing but a myth" (Karlsson 1994b).

In the spring of 1993, the conflict between the two escalated. Granted, Wachtmeister himself had threatened to overthrow the Government in the early months of the year (Neiman 1993) but as indicated above, it was Karlsson who pursued the antigovernment line the furthest. Seeing New Democracy's declining support in the polls (having fallen from 9.6 to 7.7 percent in Sifo's surveys), Karlsson stated openly that it had been a mistake to form a New Democracy party in the first place, and regretted not having continued as a pure opinion former. In expressing a desire to overthrow the Government, he was not intimating that he thought a Social Democratic Government would do the job better, but trying to demonstrate that the Social Democrats would also be incapable of holding office. As far as Karlsson was concerned, the problems facing Sweden could not be solved by the mainstream parties; what was needed was civil disobedience: "The establishment is pulling the wool over the eyes of normal citizens. What is needed is a revolution from the bottom up. Normal people must go out and protest. It is as simple as that. Civil disobedience is clearly the only option remaining" (Peruzzi 1993). When asked about his views on New Democracy's ideology, Karlsson answered that he wanted to see the party "constantly in the middle of everything."

New Democracy's conduct in connection with the way it unexpectedly voted against its own proposal on partial pensions without having prewarned anyone also provoked the threat of a new election from Prime Minister Carl Bildt. This was generally taken as being to Karlsson's credit and prompted Lars Moquist MP to write a letter to Ian Wachtmeister deploring Karlsson's behavior and accusing him of being a rabble-rouser obsessed with tactical posturing and political bluff-mongering. Moquist's letter was not intended for public consumption, but the fact that it was addressed to Wachtmeister reflects the rupture in the party between its two generals. In response to all this turmoil, Bert Karlsson threatened to withdraw from politics (Mellin 1993; Rydgren 1995).

However, it was Bildt's threat of a new election that finally made the conflict between Bert Karlsson and Ian Wachtmeister manifest. After talks with Carl Bildt, New Democracy had rescued the Government and precluded a new election and there was talk of Wachtmeister deciding thereafter to appear as a more serious and responsible politician. There is much to suggest that he never really wanted to overthrow a nonsocialist government in the first place. As already pointed out, he gave priority to the neoliberal economic-political program so it is hard to believe that he would have preferred a Social Democrat rule, and he was also probably unnerved by the unfavorable response of the market, for which the party was blamed. Once New Democracy had succeeded in blackmailing the Government to sit round the negotiating table, Wachtmeister saw no reason to keep hold of the populist antiestablishment strategy as there were superior political goals. This political U-turn did not please Karlsson, who told journalists that it was Wachtmeister's idea to support the Bildt Government, and that he himself had been browbeaten in the internal debate. He was also heard to complain about "Ian's crackpot order to support the Government at all costs" (Eneberg 1993). Unlike Wachtmeister, Karlsson had no scruples about overthrowing a nonsocialist government. The cleavage dimension he prioritized went much further beyond the realms of traditional bloc politics and was directed at the "political establishment" as a whole.

New Democracy's support continued to slide after its settlement with the Government, and in May 1993 another dispute between Wachtmeister and Karlsson shook the party once more around the proposal of increase in taxation, which Karlsson advocated and Wachtmeister resolutely opposed. Karlsson also went on to argue that the Government should pay a price for New Democracy's support, and accused Wachtmeister, who was busy reassuring the Government of the party's continued support, of being too pusillanimous to stand up to it (Ronge 1993b). Wachtmeister, in his defense, argued that it was important to be able to choose among different political packages and said that he was not prepared to support the Social Democrats on certain issues as their political package was worse than that of the Government (*Svenska Dagbladet*, 7 May 1993). This also suggests that Wachtmeister had partially abandoned the populist strategy, which necessitates compliance with the prevailing public opinion on any one issue. This time too we can trace the cause of the split between the two men to their differences of opinion as regards the populist antiestablishment strategy; nor can we rule out the possibility that their antagonism was exacerbated by their opposing political views, which emanated from different ideological positions along the right-left dimension. We could also talk of a conflict between the right (Wachtmeister) and left (Karlsson) flanks of the party. After all, the latter had once said in a newspaper interview that deep down he was really a Social Democrat (*Skånska Dagbladet*, 24 February 1992).

At the same time, such remarks, like the call for increased taxation, can be seen as a desire to follow a changing public opinion. When New Democracy was formed and its manifesto drawn up, there was, as we have seen, a socioeconomic right-wing wind on the voter arena. New Democracy's neoliberal right-wing populism was therefore in alignment with the mood of the general public. During its Riksdag term, again as we have seen, public opinion shifted to the left. It is reasonable to assume that Bert Karlsson simply wanted to follow this leftist orientation and move his party's footing accordingly along the economic right-left dimension. His rhetoric during the later months of New Democracy's Riksdag term was as much left-wing populist as it was right-wing populist (seen from a socioeconomic perspective), albeit combined with an ever more austere anti-immigrant/immigration polemic. This slide to the left in Karlsson's populism is illustrated by the following quote, in which he states explicitly that he was not prepared to go along with the party's policy of privatization:

> I still believe in making cuts in the public sector, but for me it went without saying that they were to be made to the bureaucracy and to the political administration, not by firing the carers and the teachers. In my opinion, we need to make savings in local government, but not by making people unemployed and pushing them over to another account—unemployment benefit. Worse healthcare and worse schooling without any definite savings does not agree with common sense (Karlsson 1994a).

However, Wachtmeister possessed no sympathy for such a change in direction, nor did those recruited from his own circles. They were ideologically shaped by the neoliberal SAF policy of the 1980s and were unable and/or unwilling to follow public opinion for strategic purposes. Nor did Wachtmeister show any signs of being prepared to abandon the party's political program, which such a change would entail. In this conflict we find much of what caused the two men to go their separate ways.

In the autumn of 1993, the relationship between them deteriorated even more. In November, following a Sifo survey that had the party plummet from 11 percent in June 1992 to 4.4 percent in October 1993, Karlsson went public with his criticism of Wachtmeister: "Ian rejects referenda, and is the biggest crocodile of all. He sees blue when negotiating with the social democrats and [the Social Democratic party leader] Ingvar Carlsson has a point in saying that Ian might as well join the Government" (Ronge 1993b). Karlsson continued to mudsling Wachtmeister into the winter, accusing him of "sitting in the Government's lap" (Björk 1994). In early February 1994, the conflict between the two came to a head. Karlsson had launched in a newspaper interview his demand that New Democracy change tactics. In order to boost their standing in the polls (which balanced precariously on the 4 percent threshold) ahead of the forthcoming election, Karlsson, feeling that the party had been far too honest and too responsible, wanted it to adopt a "policy of blackmail." He also threatened to resign if the Government's proposal on child-care allowance passed through parliament with New Democracy's backing. Wachtmeister opposed such a switch of tactics; what was of fundamental importance, he asserted, was the effect on the Swedish economy and people, and he refused to purchase poll gains with "dishonest" policies

(Leijonhufvud 1994). Karlsson was on the whole highly disgruntled over what he understood as Wachtmeister's failure to exploit the antiestablishment strategy opportunity that had presented itself:

> There is a striking similarity between the mainstream non-socialist parties and the Social Democrats. They protect the establishment and all its advantages. This is a trap I do not want to see New Democracy fall into, for then much of the point of the party would go up in smoke. So it is also important for New Democracy to be above playing along with the terms and conditions of traditional bloc politics. We must remain neutral when dealing with the blue [right] and red [left] camps and be able to vote through the best option. This is something Ian has had real problems with. He literally sees red at the idea of cooperating and doing deals with the Social Democrats. . . . People see New Democracy as a party that goes on and on about using its power to overthrow the Government but when it comes down to it supports the Government's line anyway. We are being punished by our voters because we are taking responsibility for a government's longevity and these signals I think have gone over Ian's head (Karlsson 1994a).

So yet again, we find the roots of Karlsson's umbrage in New Democracy's support for the nonsocialist government, which he felt had caused the disastrous poll results. A more radical use of the populist antiestablishment strategy was needed to turn the tide, and if this meant acting contrary to its manifesto (not least the economic-political program) so be it; or as Karlsson expressed it: "You can think the right things, but what good does that do if you are not in the Riksdag?" (Björk 1994). Wachtmeister held a different opinion. For him, certain political ambitions trumped party ratings and in the goal conflict between voter maximization and manifesto implementation (and ideological fidelity) his judgments were different from those of Karlsson, and he was not prepared to abandon his own—and thus New Democracy's—economic political creed simply to follow the changing public opinion. It is also possible that Wachtmeister disagreed about the value of using tactical blackmail and that he wanted to avoid New Democracy becoming the cause of a political and thus (in these times of economic recession) economic crisis for reasons as much ideological as strategic. New Democracy was constantly blamed for jeopardizing the country's economy in the ultimatums they regularly delivered to the Government, which on repeated occasions caused interest rates to skyrocket. The costs of using a radical "balance of power" strategy became heavier, and it is far from certain that such conduct at that time was appreciated by the voters. So the conflict between the market and the populist strategy may have restricted New Democracy's political room to maneuver. If the party forsook previous promises and deals in order to maximize votes, the market would respond negatively; interest rates would rise and the krona would depreciate. This happened when the Government threatened a new election as well as when New Democracy's support for the Government was undermined by Karlsson's tax increase maneuver. It was not good for the party to be seen as the cause of market unrest from either a strategic or an ideological perspective. Far too many people, and voters, were affected.

Only a few days after Karlsson's initiative, Wachtmeister suddenly announced that he was planning to resign at the party's general party conference that April—live on the news without a word of warning to his party colleagues. A press release from Wachtmeister explained how he felt that he had lost control over the party:

> New Democracy has changed. Now when Sweden more than ever needs tough, straight-talking parties, our forthright style is suddenly challenged— from within the party. . . . As late as this autumn I was completely prepared to continue. But time and time again I have witnessed how the party's powers of resistance have been emasculated by the Sifo polls. That is the serious thing. New Democracy should be a movement that closes ranks and grows stronger when things get tough (Jönsson 1994).

Wachtmeister was also openly disappointed with Karlsson's lack of loyalty. "When I have spent 50 hours mulling over a difficult issue, it seems terribly easy for Bert, who's spent five minutes on it after reading some evening tabloid" (Stenberg 1994). After Wachtmeister's departure, the conflict between the two became irredeemable and left no doubt that their insurmountable personal differences were very much to blame.

A matter of days after the announcement of Wachtmeister's imminent departure, Karlsson demanded that he leave the party with immediate effect. Wachtmeister wrote a letter distancing himself from New Democracy and suggesting disbandment if it failed to clear the four percent barrier in that autumn's election.

The search for Wachtmeister's successor commenced immediately since Karlsson, who declared himself incompetent as leader, declined to step in (Björk 1994). The post eventually went to Harriet Colliander (Bert Karlsson's candidate), who was voted in as the new group leader for New Democracy at the end of February (Westlind 1994). Colliander also announced that she had accepted the nomination committee's request that she become the new party chairman. Committee chairman Robert Jousma, however, claimed that she had not even been asked (Eriksson 1994) and a few days later put forward another name, Sten Dybeck, who had joined the party a few months previously. Wachtmeister backed this new nomination for chairman, while Karlsson stood firmly behind Colliander (Olofsson 1994).

Wachtmeister's resignation as group leader also marked the beginning of a new political attitude for New Democracy in the Riksdag. For instance, the party changed sides in the Standing Committee on Social Affairs and voted against the Government's Family Doctor Bill. However, the party's results continued to decline in the polls, reaching only 3.3 percent in a Sifo survey in March 1994 (Rydgren 1996: 16). As we have seen, the internal split widened after Wachtmeister's resignation, and once the mainstay, the party leader and founder, had stepped aside, the party collapsed like a house of cards. Already at the end of March 1994 there was a kind of judicial division of the party's and Riksdag group's assets (Ronge 1994). The split in the party was further aggravated by Harriet Colliander, who, after talks with Prime Minister Bildt, went against her own parliamentary group at the end of May and made a U-turn on child-care allowance with a vote of approval. Karlsson immediately broke with Colliander and announced that he wanted Vivianne Franzén as party leader. There was now talk of three different phalanxes within New Democracy: the Wachtmeister, Karlsson and Colliander factions (Pedersen 1994). In a now-rare moment of accord, Wachtmeister and Karlsson both said that they wanted to see Franzén voted in as the new party chairman at the extra party conference in June—which she duly was. A malcontent old executive committee claimed that the extra party conference had no mandate to elect a new one and appealed the decision, blocking the new party executive with no access to the party funds (Karlsson 1994). Nevertheless, Franzén went on to be elected in the members' ballot on June 21, a victory that incited Colliander to announce her resignation the following day (Alfredsson 1994).

The 1994 election campaign was also completely colored by the internal rifts. In early July 1994, the Stockholm District Court ruled that Franzén's election was invalid (Eriksson 1994). She accordingly withdrew from the party's campaign, saying that she was not prepared to do anything until she had been formally elected as the legitimate leader, which was expected to happen at the extra party conference on 20 August (i.e., a month before the general election). In the vacuum left by Franzén, Gunilla Aastrup Persson declared herself "acting" party leader and the new party chairman. These two were then joined by Bert Karlsson, who also put his name down as a candidate for party leader at the party conference in August. The vote finally went to Franzén (Svenska Dagbladet, 21 August 1994). After this tumultuous campaign, during which Karlsson accused New Democracy of appearing more and more as "a Labor Market Board project for dogmatists and nutcases" (Karlsson 1994b), New Democracy managed to scrape together no more than 1.2 percent of the vote in the general election of 18 September and disappeared from the Riksdag after only one term on the backbenches. The process of disintegration continued at an accelerating pace, swiftly reducing the party to a sect-like club until it vanished from the scene altogether.

Problems on the parliamentary arena

It was not only the goal conflict between the voter arena and the internal arena that affected New Democracy during its parliamentary term, but also that between the voter arena and the parliamentary arena.

Before the 1991 election, New Democracy had plans to hold the balance of power, a strategy in line with the populist antiestablishment strategy and one that helped the party to escape being pinioned by the goal conflict between the voter arena and the parliamentary arena (see chapter 2). The outcome of the election gave New Democracy this very position, and in order to exploit such a position to the full a party needs to be ready and able to vote with both the Government and the opposition. From the very beginning, New Democracy had made clear its intention not to be a passive Government supporter (which was reflected in the fact that the party abstained from voting when Carl Bildt was elected Prime Minister). By opposing a number of issues the party tried to force the Government to the negotiating table and in doing so use its position to realize as many as possible of its own policies. For the first year of its parliamentary term New Democracy opposed in this way the Government's proposals on a deferred increase in child allowance and the abolition of partial pensions, although it backtracked on the former after witnessing the massive impact it had on interest rates (which rose dramatically after every sign of parliamentary crisis). Again in August 1992 the party announced its intentions to veto three key Government proposals: the introduction of a qualifying day in the health insurance system, child-care allowance, and the family doctor reform. Their purpose here too was no doubt to exploit the fact that they wielded the balance of power and to force the Government into a position of compromise. The strategy failed, and instead of appealing to New Democracy, the Government, faced with a deteriorating currency crisis, cut a broad settlement with the Social Democrats.

This crisis pact between the Government and the Social Democrats temporarily deprived New Democracy of the balance of power and with it, the party's influence over Swedish politics. Equally important, if not more so, the party found itself outside the media glare during this period, and in the months following the crisis agreement between the Government and the Social Democrats New Democracy seldom attracted media attention. These events gave the first indications of the inherent weakness in New Democracy's organization. Once in the media shadow, it was obvious that the party had few alternative resources for political mobilization, an insight that doubtlessly intimidated many party members (not least Bert Karlsson). Support for New Democracy in the polls was at its highest (12.5 percent) when the nonsocialist government was forced to collaborate with the party, while it decreased substantially when the Government appealed to the Social Democrats for support (Gardberg 1993: 51). The settlement between the Government and the Social Democrats—combined with the fact that it started to become obvious that the economic crisis was upon the country—marked the start of an irreversible decline in popular support for New Democracy, and even its repossession of the balance of power after the Government's decision to float the currency had undermined the relations with the Social Democrats was unable to save it.

In January 1993, New Democracy threatened to bring down the Government if it refused to discuss the entire budget with the party, and explained that they were not prepared to vote for the Government's proposal without some sort of quid pro quo. In March 1993, the party also defeated the Government on partial pensions by voting against their own proposal at the eleventh hour in favor of the Social Democrats. Bildt then threatened to resign, which, as we have already seen, prompted Wachtmeister to pledge the party's support. This heralded the start of a period of greater responsibility in which New Democracy, by choosing sides in favor of the Government, voluntarily softened its balance-of-power posture. In so doing it limited its political room for maneuver and, as we have seen, made it impossible for the party to employ the populist antiestablishment strategy with any credibility.

Less room for maneuver

If the rise of New Democracy can be understood as the outcome of (1) its leaders' extremely authoritarian rule over the rest of the party organization (i.e., the lack of internal democracy), (2) the presence of external resources (especially the media), which made it less reliant on party members, and (3) the credible use of the populist antiestablishment strategy, its "fall" can in many respects be attributed to the same factors.

Let us begin with the third point. The populist antiestablishment strategy was, then, one of the main causes of New Democracy's emergence and success in the 1991 general election, mainly because it allowed the party to mobilize voters who had little faith in politicians and

because it guaranteed that the party could follow public opinion on individual issues. Being able to adapt to what the voters think is naturally
important to all parties in Sweden, but it was especially so to New Democracy. Already from day one the party had profiled itself as a voters'
party, and unlike the mainstream parties had no core voter group, leaving it reliant on the floating voters. During their parliamentary term,
however, a conflict arose between the voter arena and New Democracy's
internal arena, as we have seen. The party was no longer a novelty, and
a tradition of political causes had been created. In combination with
the party manifesto, this tradition helped to create a "path dependency"
for the party, which it could not simply deviate from without inciting
protest from members who identified strongly with the original manifesto clauses. The types of conflict inherent to all parties also thus appeared within New Democracy, which lacked the organizational tools to
deal with them effectively. The fact that the party had two leaders (and
founders), who identified with different manifesto items and disagreed
about strategies, simply exacerbated matters. It proved even harder for
the party to keep itself outside Swedish bloc politics (which the populist
strategy demanded) since there were clearly considerable costs associated with bringing down a nonsocialist government: the resentment of
party members and voters who valued the party's neoliberal economic-
political program, and the adverse response of the market, which hit
many voters personally. All this made it hard for New Democracy to use
the populist antiestablishment strategy in the same way as prior to the
1991 election. New Democracy thus found itself with less freedom of
movement—and less popular appeal.

As we have seen, the New Democracy executive tried to get round this
goal conflict by turning the party into a purely national party. By shrinking the internal arena so that it encompassed the national organization
only, they tried to mitigate the conflict between the voter arena and the
internal arena. The new order gave the party executive, especially Ian
Wachtmeister and Bert Karlsson, greater room for maneuver to pursue
the party's policies with impunity (and to avoid taking responsibility for
the dubious remarks of local politicians who had ended up on the ballot papers without anyone having had time to check their conduct and
moral credentials). The problems with this kind of voter party, which
prioritizes the voters at the expense of the members, are that it is heavily
dependent on strong leadership and that, due to the lack of a membership base, it inevitably stakes its existence on the support of the voters
and on the attention of the media. It is unlikely that such an organization
can survive a governmental term outside the parliament, as for instance
the Green Party did between 1991 and 1994. There was, for instance, no

established network of local organizations that could mobilize activists to continue working for the party until the leadership crisis was resolved (see Svåsand & Wølund 2001: 14). Karlsson admitted later that the decision to divorce the local branches from the party was a failure: "This is when the real disintegration starts. Ian made ambitious party colleagues feel that they had been divided up into an A and a B team" (Karlsson 1994b). As Zald and Ash (1966: 333) have pointed out, it is also hard to keep the party members motivated if they feel they have no chances of rising within the organization. And as is the case for all "charismatic" parties (see chapter 3), there are dangers associated with excessive personal importance, and organizations in which certain members are considered indispensable find it hard to survive for any length of time (Ahrne 1994). Karlsson and (in particular) Wachtmeister were virtually irreplaceable, and the party's reorganization simply served to accentuate this. Not only were there far too few differences between person and position, the party also happened to have (unlike other typical "charismatic" parties) *two* leaders. The organizational form chosen necessitates a strong leadership all working for the same ends, which as we have seen, was not the case with Karlsson and Wachtmeister after the 1991 election. New Democracy's organizational form therefore probably benefited the party while it possessed a strong leadership, but left it especially vulnerable when rifts appeared between its two leaders and, in particular, when one of them (Wachtmeister) handed in his resignation.

New Democracy's problems within its own parliamentary group can also be largely reduced to its peculiar organizational form. The many defections can be put down to the lack of a coherent ideological glue, the result of the manner in which its MPs were appointed autocratically by the executive rather than democratically by the members. Since the party was newly formed at the time of the general election, the opportunities for internal recruitment were small, and there was neither the time nor the will to instruct New Democracy's candidates in the field of politics through internal party work, which usually serves to sift out less suitable candidates before they reach the nomination stage and which was not the case for New Democracy. The upshot of all this was that the party group acted with little discipline, and without a fairly unified party group, Riksdag parties function poorly (New Democracy, for instance, failed on several occasions to keep its members in line at the parliamentary ballot box). This sudden goal conflict was costly for New Democracy, and one that it was organizationally ill-equipped to remove painlessly.

After Wachtmeister's resignation, New Democracy lost cohesion. General party conferences were plagued by infighting, and the Riksdag group failed to maintain a unified party line at voting times. The most likely reasons for this disarray were its organizational form, which was unable to accommodate Wachtmeister's departure, and the lack of a binding ideology and common history. What had been a precondition of its rapid growth and success in the 1991 election proved ultimately to be its undoing.

New Democracy's strategy of relying on the media as an external resource for disseminating its political message also proved vulnerable during the party's term in the parliament, and the party disappeared in the media shadow for two lengthy periods of time. The first was in connection with the crisis settlement between the Government and the Social Democrats, which deprived New Democracy of the balance of power, and the second was when this power position was voluntarily relinquished after Carl Bildt's threat to resign and call a new election, which reduced New Democracy to a relatively obedient support party for Government (thus rendering it of little interest to the media). This also heralded the first real signs of what proved to be an irreversible decline in the opinion polls for New Democracy (Rydgren 1995: 48).

Notes

1. The figures quoted here refer to 1991–1994.

5

WHY HAS THERE BEEN NO SUCCESSFUL SWEDISH RRP PARTY SINCE 1994?

Since the collapse of New Democracy in 1994, no Swedish (radical) right-wing populist party has come close to winning a parliamentary seat. Even given the relative success of the today's leading RRP party, the Sweden Democrats, in the 2002 general election (in which it received 1.4 percent of the vote and more than forty seats on different local councils), Sweden's RRP parties are marginalized in a Western European perspective.

This chapter, like the previous two, will follow the model laid out in chapter 2. It will thus open with a discussion on the presence of niches and other political opportunity structures for the development of (radical) right-wing populist parties on the Swedish political arena since 1994. It will then address the question of why no RRP party has established itself in the country during this time, when such parties have been successful in most other Western European countries. Next, we will turn to a discussion of the Sweden Democrats: to what extent has the party made use of the populist antiestablishment strategy and ethnopluralist nationalism (and other effective rhetorical tools for mobilizing anti-immigrant voters)? And how successful have they been in presenting themselves as credible and in promulgating their message? In finding an answer to these questions, we shall also be taking a closer look at the Sweden Democrats' party organization.

Political opportunity structures

As we have seen, the number of vacant niches on the electoral arena was dramatically changed as a result of the socioeconomic shift to the left in the early and mid 1990s. Since 1995, however, the electorate has been relatively evenly distributed over the left-right divide, with some 32–34 percent identifying as "left" and equally many as "right." In 2002, there was a new shift to the left, pushing the proportion of voters identifying themselves as left wing up to 40 percent, while the proportion of voters considering themselves "right" stayed put at 32 percent. This can thus be seen as a sign of increased polarization (Holmberg & Weibull 2003a: 15). Since the mid 1990s, attitudes toward the public sector have largely remained unchanged, although a slight decline can be noted. In 2002, 39 percent of the voters opposed cuts in the public sector, down from 49 percent in 1996; on the other hand, public support for such a measure rose from 23 to 28 percent from 1996 to 2002 (Nilsson 2003: 61). This leads us to conclude that the chances of a "neoliberal" party emerging today are much smaller than they were back when New Democracy became established in the early 1990s. This fact cannot, however, explain the Sweden Democrats' lack of success as it, like most other contemporary Western European RRP parties, has a deliberately more middle-of-the-road socioeconomic profile as a champion of the welfare state.

Although there have also been changes to the two remaining niches (anti-immigrant/immigration and political discontent), there is theoretical room for the emergence of a successful Swedish RRP party nonetheless. However, we shall leave this discussion until later. Before proceeding, I will give a brief account of the economic factors that previous research has identified as responsible for the growth of RRP parties (see chapter 2).

First, there can be no doubt that over the past few decades, the Swedish economy has joined others in its transition from industrialism to postindustrialism, and as we have already discussed, service production has mushroomed at the expense of goods production: a key indicator of postindustrialization. Second, during the 1990s Sweden suffered an economic crisis at least as deep as in other Western European countries. A subjective indicator of this is that the number of voters who believed that the "economy has got worse" between 1990 and 1997 far outstripped the number of those who thought it had improved, and this in terms of both the national economy and their own financial situation (Holmberg 2000: 141; Holmberg & Weibull 2003: 11).

In the mid 1990s, and to a certain extent later than this, a large proportion of the Swedish electorate thus considered themselves personally worse off, creating a situation in Sweden that is normally seen as a breeding ground for the growth of RRP parties. Such feelings of relative deprivation peaked around the middle of the decade, but started to improve by the turn of the millennium.

The level of unemployment is also taken to be of particular importance in this context, given the frustration and social unease that it breeds. Table 5.1, which gives levels of unemployment in thirteen Western European countries between 1992 and 2000, however, shows that there was no strong, unequivocal relationship between unemployment and the presence or strength of RRP parties. Finland (for whom the 1990s were marked by a total lack of RRP parties) had the highest unemployment figures of all, while Austria, where one of Europe's most successful RRP parties has been making remarkable progress, had the lowest. Comparing Sweden with the countries in which an RRP has a presence, we find that unemployment was lower than in Italy, France, and Belgium, but higher than in Denmark and Austria. We also know that unemployment in Sweden increased in the early 1990s from 3 percent (Holmberg & Weibull 1999: 24) at the start of the decade, to 5.8 percent two years later, and 9.9 percent just one year after that (see Table 5.1). But here too, as Table 5.1 shows, the situation has recovered since 1998.

Given that young voters are overrepresented among RRP parties' supporters, we could assume that youth unemployment has particularly strong impact on their development. Table 5.2, which gives unemployment figures for people below twenty-five years of age, follows, however, the same pattern as Table 5.1. It is actually even more difficult to trace a strong, unequivocal relationship between youth unemployment and the presence/strength of RRP parties. We also find that the average unemployment rate for young people was 17.0 percent between 1992 and 2000, peaking between 1993 and 1994 at 22.6 percent, and not falling below that 20 percent mark until 1997. There were, then, even in these terms, conditions that would favor the emergence of an electorally successful Swedish (radical) right-wing populist party. This was also true even after New Democracy's departure in 1994.

We can safely infer from all this that Sweden was by no means spared the great depression and unemployment of the 1990s. We have also seen how the relationship between unemployment and the presence/strength of RRP parties is, if it exists at all, clearly weak at best. However, we also saw that the economic situation in the country was at its worst in the early to mid 1990s. The deterioration of the Swedish economy, and the consequent rise in unemployment, was, nevertheless, at its most dramatic between 1991 and 1994, a period during which New Democracy already had a presence in the Swedish parliament—even if the party's voter support declined rapidly after the fall of 1992 (Rydgren 1995; Statistics Sweden 1994). Yet these circumstances are equally unable to explain why no new RRP party became established in the years to follow, before the economy started to recover properly.

Table 5.1. Unemployment rates in Europe, 1992–2000

	Mean 92–00	1992	1993	1994	1995	1996	1997	1998	1999	2000 (Jan.)
1. Spain	20.1	18.5	22.8	24.1	22.9	22.2	20.8	18.8	15.9	15.1
2. Finland	13.8	13.0	17.7	17.9	16.6	14.6	12.7	11.4	10.2	10.2
3. France	11.6	10.4	11.7	12.3	11.6	12.4	12.3	11.8	11.3	10.5
4. Italy	11.2	9.0	10.3	11.4	11.9	12.0	12.0	11.9	11.3	11.2
5. Ireland	10.8	15.4	15.6	14.3	12.4	11.7	9.9	7.6	5.7	5.0
6. Belgium	9.2	7.3	8.9	10.0	9.9	9.7	9.4	9.5	9.0	8.7
7. Germany	8.5	6.6	7.9	8.4	8.2	8.9	9.9	9.4	8.7	8.5
8. Sweden	**8.5**	**5.8**	**9.9**	**9.8**	**9.2**	**9.6**	**9.9**	**8.3**	**7.2**	**6.6**
9. Britain	8.0	10.1	10.4	9.6	8.8	8.2	7.0	6.3	6.1	5.9
10. Denmark	6.9	9.2	10.1	8.2	7.1	6.8	5.6	5.2	5.2	5.0
11. Portugal	5.8	4.2	5.7	7.0	7.3	7.3	6.8	5.2	4.5	4.3
12. Netherlands	5.3	5.6	6.6	7.1	7.0	6.3	5.2	4.0	3.3	2.7
13. Austria	4.1	—	—	—	3.8	4.3	4.4	4.5	3.7	3.6

Source: Eurostat (2000, 57); Eurostat (1996, 57). For Austria the mean is between based on 1995–2000.

Table 5.2. Unemployment rates in Europe, persons under twenty years of age

	Mean 92–00	1992	1993	1994	1995	1996	1997	1998	1999	2000 (Jan.)
1. Spain	36.7	34.6	43.4	45.0	42.5	41.9	38.9	35.4	29.5	27.9
2. Italy	32.0	27.1	30.4	32.3	33.2	33.5	33.1	33.8	32.7	31.8
3. Finland	30.6	32.6	41.8	42.2	38.2	28.0	25.2	23.5	21.4	22.5
4. France	26.3	23.3	27.3	29.0	27.3	29.1	29.2	26.3	23.6	21.5
5. Belgium	22.7	16.2	21.8	24.2	24.4	23.2	23.1	23.1	24.7	23.5
6. *Sweden*	*17.9*	*13.6*	*22.6*	*22.6*	*19.4*	*20.5*	*20.6*	*16.6*	*13.6*	*12.0*
7. Ireland	16.9	24.4	25.2	22.8	19.5	18.2	15.4	11.3	8.3	6.9
8. Britain	15.2	16.7	17.9	17.0	15.9	15.5	14.2	13.6	13.0	12.7
9. Portugal	12.8	10.1	12.9	15.1	16.6	16.8	15.1	10.6	9.0	9.3
10. Denmark	10.3	12.7	13.8	11.0	10.1	10.6	8.4	7.9	9.7	8.5
11. Netherlands	9.4	8.5	11.1	11.4	11.6	11.7	9.5	8.0	7.2	5.4
12. Germany	8.9	6.4	7.9	8.7	8.8	10.0	10.8	9.9	9.0	8.9
13. Austria	5.8	—	—	—	5.6	6.2	6.7	6.4	5.0	4.7

Source: Eurostat (2000, 58); Eurostat (1996, 58). For Austria the mean is based on 1995–2000.

Political discontent and more political mobility—but maintained class voting

As we will recall from chapter 2, political discontent and alienation are two of the root causes of RRP party growth. Combined, they are considered the most critical negative factor, in the sense that political discontent pushes voters away from the mainstream parties, freeing up resources for new parties in the process (Rydgren 2003b: chapter 6). Political discontent and alienation can have both a direct and an indirect effect by sowing the seeds of political protest (in itself a fundamental condition for the emergence of all kinds of protest party) and by releasing voters from their ties with the mainstream parties (one of the conditions for the appearance of new parties generally). In this respect, the declining degrees of party identification and of class voting are particularly important.

Throughout history, and in all democracies, there have always been people who are unhappy with the political system and its institutions (Mény & Surel 2000: 23). The extent and depth of this displeasure has, however, not remained constant—not least in Sweden. Over the past few decades, confidence in the political establishment and in politicians has dwindled in the majority of Western European democracies. In a study covering Western Europe, the U.S.A. and Japan, Robert Putnam and colleagues found that confidence in politicians has declined in twelve of the thirteen countries studied; meanwhile public confidence in parliament has similarly dropped in eleven out of fourteen countries (Putnam et al. 2000: 19). As we can see in Table 5.3, political institutions enjoy the lowest public confidence of all public institutions, and by far the lowest ranking of these are the political parties.

And in this respect Sweden is no exception; in fact, confidence in political institutions has declined more in Sweden since the end of the 1960s than in most other European countries (Möller 2000: 52). In saying this, however, we should not forget that before the decline started, public confidence in the political establishment was, from both a national and a global perspective, exceptionally high in Sweden (Holmberg & Weibull 1997: 79).

Whatever the situation, Swedish voters now have little respect for political institutions. As we can see in Table 5.4, Sweden's political establishment is also the least confidence inspiring. In 2002, a mere 1 percent of those polled had full confidence in political parties, and 13 percent fairly high confidence (not shown in the table). Little or no confidence in political parties, on the other hand, was expressed by no less than 41 percent of the voters (Holmberg & Weibull 2003b: 44). This

Table 5.3. Confidence in societal institutions in Europe, 1998

Respondents with confidence (in %)	European Union	France	Germany	Italy	UK
The government	*37*	*37*	*29*	*27*	*46*
The parliament	*40*	*38*	*35*	*29*	*46*
The political parties	*16*	*12*	*13*	*13*	*18*
The church	50	36	47	55	54
The legal system	43	36	50	31	48
The unions	38	36	39	29	36
The press	40	51	42	34	15
The radio	63	62	62	49	67
The television	56	46	59	42	65

Source: Ménu & Surel (2000, 159), based on European Union's 1998 Euro barometer.

pattern was echoed in the statistics for the country's national politicians: 2 percent of the voters stated that they had strong confidence and 27 percent that they had rather strong confidence in national politicians (Holmberg & Weibull 2003b: 56).

Table 5.4. Confidence in political institutions in Sweden, 1996 and 1998

Institution	Very high		Rather high		Rather low		Neither high nor low		Very low	
	1996	2000	1996	2000	1996	2000	1996	2000	1996	2000
The parliament	3	2	16	25	39	45	25	18	17	9
The government	2	3	16	14	35	40	27	22	20	11
The local governments	2	2	13	18	40	47	28	24	17	9
Political parties	—	1	—	13	—	45	—	30	—	14

Source: Holmberg & Weibull (1997: 81); Holmberg & Weibull (2001: 29).

Despite these trends, we can also observe how voters in Sweden have become all the more pleased with how democracy in the country operates. As we can see in Table 5.5, Swedes were no more satisfied than other Western Europeans around the mid 1990s. They were, in fact, much less satisfied than their Danish counterparts and were roughly on the same level as the French or Austrians (i.e., electorates that had voted in powerful RRP parties). However, from the mid 1990s to 2002, the proportion of voters who claimed to be "very or fairly pleased with democracy in Sweden" increased to 74 percent, making the Swedish voters among the most contented in Europe, at least as regards the democratic process (Holmberg & Weibull 2003: 13). This suggests, therefore, that in recent years the niche for the mobilization of discontent has contracted.[1]

Table 5.5. Level of satisfaction with the functioning of democracy, spring 1996

Question: "On the whole, are you very satisfied, fairly satisfied, not very satisfied, or not at all satisfied with the way the democracy works (in your country)?"

Country:	Very or fairly satisfied (in percent)
1. Denmark	84 percent
2. Ireland	70 percent
3. Netherlands	64 percent
4. Finland	63 percent
5. UK	61 percent
6. Germany (west)	57 percent
7. Sweden	*55 percent*
8. Austria	53 percent
9. Spain	52 percent
10. France	51 percent
11. Portugal	49 percent
12. Belgium	45 percent
13. Germany (east)	39 percent
14. Italy	20 percent

Source: Holmberg (1997: 338).

Having said this, people expressed considerable displeasure with (established) politicians and political parties. Public agreement with the statement "The Riksdag does not care very much about what normal people think," for instance, increased from 46 percent in 1968 to 60 percent in 1982, and again to 75 percent in 1998. Similarly, belief that "The parties are interested in people's votes, not their opinions" also rose from 37 percent to 68 percent in 1991 and to 75 percent in 1998 (Holmberg 2000: 34).

However, we ought not to forget that support for democratic principles remains firm (see also Norris 1999). In 1994, a full 93 percent of Swedish voters believed that democracy is the ideal political system. This is high compared to the rest of Western Europe, which at the time varied between 74 and 93 percent (Dalton 1999: 70; Klingemann 1999: 44).

To sum up, then, there is and has been a considerable, albeit limited, scope for protest mobilization for a populist party through the incitement of popular discontent with the mainstream political establishment—provided that it is not perceived as challenging democratic principles. This situation also implies that more voters have been released from their political loyalties, and thus are available for voter mobilization on the electoral arena. That this is the case is even more obvious when we consider the declining degree of party identification.

As mentioned above, party identification and class voting are two key indicators of political stability. The term "party identification" denotes the psychological affiliation an individual has for a certain party (Campbell et al. 1960). Even though such identification can vary in strength, it is usually assumed that it constitutes a relatively stable factor in the voting patterns found within any political system. One could say, by way of slight oversimplification, that voters with a strong party identification will always vote for the party with which they identify, assuming that nothing out of the ordinary provokes them to do otherwise.

Traditionally speaking, party identification has always had a powerful influence on voter behavior. However, the number of voters with strong party identification has declined in Western Europe in recent decades (Putnam et al. 2000: 17); so too in Sweden, where figures dropped from 53 percent in 1960, to 34 percent in 1982 and 21 percent in 1991, reaching 19 percent in 1998 (Holmberg 2000: 41). In consequence, Swedish voters have become increasingly mobile, with voters shifting from one party to another increasing dramatically. In 1998 30.7 percent of the voters voted for another party than what they did in the previous election in 1994, which should be compared to 20.2 percent shifting party between 1985 and 1988. In a similar way, the proportion of voters stating that they did not decide how to vote until the election campaign (roughly speaking until one month before the election) also increased over these ten years from 40 percent 1988 to 57 percent 1998 (Holmberg 2000: 19–22).

Class voting is also a relatively stable factor in the understanding of voter behavior. In general, class voting occurs when people who belong to the same class vote, statistically speaking, in the same way. It can be seen as an expression of their common interests, which are based on common socioeconomic life conditions (see, e.g., Nieuwbeerta & De Graf 1999).

Class voting, as measured by the Alford index, has experienced a widespread decline in Western Europe, including Sweden (see Table 5.6). Swedish class voting was, however, unusually high before the trend turned downward, and is still well above that of many other countries. It should also be pointed out that this trend did not continue into the 1990s, and that class voting is still high for working-class voters (albeit slightly less than during the 1990s): of all the industrial workers in the country, 75 percent voted for either the Social Democrats or the Left Party in the 1998 election. The figure for other workers was 63 percent (Holmberg 2000: 68).

Table 5.6. Levels of class voting (measured by Alford Index)

	1945–1960	1961–1970	1971–1980	1981–1990
Austria	—	29.3	28.3	18.3
Belgium	—	25.4	17.9	16.4
Britain	37.3	38.3	24.3	23.4
Denmark	39.8	52.0	28.1	20.9
Finland	48.4	50.2	36.9	35.7
France	24.4	18.3	17.0	11.7
Germany	36.0	24.8	14.9	13.4
Italy	26.6	14.5	17.8	13.1
Netherlands	14.0	14.7	21.8	15.5
Norway	52.5	32.0	33.8	20.5
Sweden	51.0	40.7	37.3	32.7

Source: Nieuwbeerta (2001: 126). The index score is obtained by taking the difference between the percentage of manual voters that voted for left-wing political parties and the percentage of nonmanual workers that voted for these parties.

This is important, since we know from previous studies that working-class voters are one of the groups overrepresented among the supporters of RRP parties (cf. Rydgren 2003b: chapter 2; Betz 1994). Having said this, the proportion of abstainers is also high in this group: 26 percent of industrial workers and 23 percent of other workers abstained from voting in the 1998 election, along with no less than 40 percent of the unemployed (Holmberg 2000: 68, 100). Voting apathy was also high among the young, another group that is generally overrepresented in terms of RRP support. In the 1998 general election, 28 percent of the voters below 21 years of age and 25 percent of the 22–30 years cohort abstained from voting (Holmberg 2000: 82).

Again, we find that Sweden is no exception when it comes to party identification. However, the picture for class voting is more ambitious. Even though class voting has declined in Sweden, it remains fairly high, especially among the working classes, and this can obstruct the emergence of a strong Swedish RRP party. Moreover, this and the fact that union membership in Sweden is higher than in any other EU country (Ebbinghaus & Visser 2000; Kjellberg 2000) suggest that there is still a relatively strong sense of class affinity in Sweden. In fact, the proportion of manual workers who identified themselves with the working class was slightly higher (53.6 percent) in 1995 than it was in 1980 (Sohlberg & Leiulfsrud 2000: 54). This indicates that "traditionally provided and sustained collective identities" have not been eroded or destroyed in Sweden to the extent that Betz (1994: 29) claims, and that the socioeconomic cleavage dimension still dominates Swedish politics.

There are possible historical reasons for Sweden's exceptionally high class voting. Lipset (in Mair et al. 1999: 313) has, for instance, shown that the complexity of the cleavage structure has had a considerable impact. In certain countries, like France and Belgium, there have always been other cleavage dimensions of weight (such as religion, ethnicity, urban/rural) that have cut across class loyalties. There, the importance of the economic conflict dimension declined more rapidly. Sweden, on the other hand, has always had a relatively simple cleavage structure in which the economic dimension has been heavily dominant and class loyalties strong.

So what about the "new underclass" that Betz (1994) identifies as the result of the structural transition from an industrial to a postindustrial economy? Is it not mainly among the old, well-established trades and jobs where feelings of class affinity, perhaps even loyalty, remain? This is indeed possible, in which case it is likely that a significant proportion of the "new underclass" can be found among the abstainers (which is partly suggested by the very high incidence of voter apathy among the unemployed). It is therefore possible that the "new underclass" category of the Swedish electorate has so far opted for "exit" over "voice" as a reaction to their growing marginalization (Hirschman 1970). However, we should not completely rule out the possibility that an emerging protest party (such as an RRP party) would have the capacity to change this inclination.

We should also stress that for a large proportion of the electorate, class affinity or party identification have no effect on voting behavior. Moreover, a growing number of voters abstain from voting, not least those who in other countries have had a penchant for RRP parties, such as workers, the unemployed, and voters below 30 years of age. During the 1998 general election, 18 percent of industrial workers and 21 percent of the lower nonmanual workers admitted to having no preference for any particular party (Holmberg 2000: 45). This indicates that there is room for a new party, possibly an RRP party, to establish itself, especially bearing in mind that 52 percent of the abstainers (as opposed to 43 percent of all voters) believed it a good idea to "bring fewer asylum seekers into the country" (Holmberg 2000: 133). From this, we can conclude that some 10 percent of the electorate in the 1998 election abstained from voting while simultaneously sharing anti-asylum seeker sentiments. This could be a potential niche favoring the emergence of an electorally successful Swedish RRP party.

Political issues: Immigration and the EU

Sweden has long been a country of net immigration, in that more people have migrated in than migrated out. Non-European immigration increased in the 1970s, 1980s, and 1990s, and the figures show that during the last of these decades, the average number of asylum applications was 29 for every 1,000 Swedish citizens, as opposed to 18 in Belgium, 16 in Austria, 5 in France, and 1 in Italy (van Holsteyn & Rydgren 2004). Thus, as Kitschelt has shown, immigration per se cannot serve as an explanation for why RRP parties have become successful in some countries but failed in others (Kitschelt 1995: 62).

As discussed in earlier chapters, the prominence of immigration as an issue and the fact that the majority, or nearly so, of people in most Western European countries hold anti-immigration beliefs (Betz 1994: 103; EUMC 2001) have both been critical to the RRP parties by virtue of their mobilizing and catalytic powers (see also Kitschelt 1995: 103, 276). In other words, even though the RRP parties should not be treated as one-issue parties focusing only on immigration (Mudde

1999), xenophobia still constitutes their sine qua non. Although not all voters sharing anti-immigrant and/or xenophobic attitudes vote for RRP parties, almost all those who actually vote for such parties have such attitudes (Mayer 1999; Rydgren 2003b).

As we can see in Table 5.7, a majority of Swedish voters in the 1990s were in favor of reducing the number of asylum-seekers. Such attitudes peaked at 65 percent in 1992, falling steadily thereafter for the remainder of the decade. In 2002, however, the number of anti-immigrant voters rose once more from 44 percent to 50 percent (Demker 2003: 85). Data from the International Social Survey Program also shows that in 1995 Swedish voters were roughly just as opposed to immigrants/immigration as those in the rest of Western Europe. They were also more inclined than the average European to agree with the statement "Immigration causes crime" and just as likely to agree with the statement "Immigrants contribute nothing to the economy." A survey carried out by the EUMC (the European Monitoring Center on Racism and Xenophobia) in Vienna shows that things had changed little by 2000 (van Holsteyn & Rydgren 2004; EUMC 2001: 37–40).

The perceived importance of the immigration issue increased in the 1980s and 1990s in most Western European countries (Solomos & Wrench 1993: 4). As Table 5.8 shows, this trend peaked in Sweden in 1993, when 25 percent of the voters ranked immigration among the top three most urgent issues facing the country. The political salience of immigration then declined for the remainder of the decade, and after

Table 5.7. Attitudes toward refugees and immigrants, 1990–2000

Proportion who agree (in percent):	-90	-91	-92	-93	-94	-95	-96	-97	-98	-99	-00
It is a good idea to reduce the amount of refugees accepted to come to Sweden	61	56	65	59	56	56	54	54	50	47	43
There are too many refugees living in Sweden	—	—	—	52	—	—	—	48	—	40	—
Would not like to see a relative get married with an immigrant	—	—	—	25	—	—	—	18	—	17	—

Source: Demker (2000: 62–63; 2001: 74).

Table 5.8. The most important issues, 1989–2002 (in percent)

Question: "Which question/questions do you think is/are the most important today in Sweden? Do not mention more than three issues/societal problems."

Issue:	-89	-90	-91	-92	-93	-94	-95	-96	-97	-98	-99	-00	-01	-02
Law and order	38	11	15	8	9	11	25	14	13	15	16	15	12	12
Immigration/ refugee issues	11	14	13	19	25	12	14	13	10	8	13	12	13	19

Source: Holmberg & Weibull (2003: 11).

an election campaign very much focusing on citizenship and immigration, increased again in 2002 to become the fourth most important political issue (19 percent). This was the highest ranking it had achieved since the heyday of New Democracy in 1993 (Holmberg & Weibull 2003a: 10–11).

As mentioned previously, the very existence of xenophobic attitudes does not automatically lead to the growth of an RRP party. Nor is it sufficient for the immigration issue to be considered important and prominent; it must also be seen as a *politically* important issue. This means that it must first be politicized, or "translated" into political terms. Although an issue is politicized to a certain extent when seen as important by politicians and voters alike, it is only really fully politicized when it affects their political behavior (Rydgren 2003b: chapter 2 and 6; cf. Campbell et al. 1960). By this definition, the immigration issue was not yet fully politicized in Sweden during the 1990s. As Table 5.9 shows us, it has not proved especially important (in terms of choice of party) for the Swedish electorate, possibly with the exception of 1991, when New Democracy had its electoral breakthrough. These results corroborate Oscarsson's (1998: 273–275) argument that to date the xenophobic cleavage dimension in Sweden has been ineffectual.

It might prove an interesting exercise to compare these figures with those of the French electorate, for whom immigration has been of immense political salience over the past fifteen years. From 1986 to 1997, between 22 and 32 percent of French voters claimed that the issue was pivotal to their choice of party or presidential candidate (Schain 2001).

Table 5.9. Important issues for the voters' choice of party in the elections 1979–1998

Question: "If you think of the election this year, are there one or several issues that are/were important for your choice of party in the Parliament Election?" The proportion of voters who mentioned the following issues (on an open question), in percent.

Issue:	1979	1982	1985	1988	1991	1994	1998
Occupation/ employment	18	29	25	5	23	41	34
Welfare issues, social policy, health care	4	12	19	15	22	21	28
Pensions	5	8	8	9	20	9	17
Taxes	17	8	20	19	18	9	17
Economy	9	14	14	8	20	30	14
European Union	0	0	0	1	10	14	6
Immigration and refugee issues	*0*	*0*	*1*	*2*	*8*	*5*	*3*
Law and order	1	1	0	1	3	1	2

Source: Holmberg (2000, 114). It should be noted that these statistics exclude those who abstained from voting.

We have thus found that Sweden has about as many xenophobic and immigration-skeptic voters, per head of population, as other Western European countries; some 50 percent of the voters favor taking in fewer asylum-seekers into the country, and a relatively large proportion of voters give high priority to the issue of asylum and immigration. As Demker (2003: 89) has shown, the proportion of voters holding anti-immigrant sentiments was higher (60 percent) among those who ranked refugee and immigration issues among the top three social problems. This means that 11 percent of the voters want a tighter immigration and asylum policy *and* consider this issue more important than most other issues. It is among such voters that the RRP parties can hope to mobilize support, leaving us to conclude that there is a relatively large niche for a Swedish anti-immigration/immigrant party, such as an RRP party, to take root. At the same time, however, immigration has not been such an important and salient *political* issue, in the sense that it affects people's voting behavior, as it has been in the countries where RRP parties have enjoyed a measure of success, and this helps to curb such developments. Since the 1994 election, immigration has more or less disappeared from the list of issues affecting voter choice, with a reservation for the 2002 election for which data are still unavailable. We must, however, be careful in determining causality here, as there are indications that such issues only become fully prioritized *after* an RRP party has become established (Rydgren 2003a).

As discussed in preceding chapters, there is much to suggest (see also Table 5.5) that the economic crisis in Sweden boosted the relative importance of conventional issues of political economy and the welfare state rather than those of a sociocultural nature, such as immigration and law and order. While questions of the economy and employment dominated the crisis years around the mid 1990s, health care and education have dominated the electorate's agenda since the end of that decade. In fact, the former has emerged as a particularly critical issue since the mid 1990s, and whereas in 1995 only 15 percent of voters gave it any serious priority, by 1999 this figure was up at 41 percent. The same can be said of education, which also soared from 7 percent in 1995 to 32 percent in 2002.

Before moving on, I will discuss briefly the politicization of the EU issue, in particular the 1994 referendum. We know from previous studies that many RRP parties have succeeded in turning EU opposition to their advantage, attracting voters by linking EU opposition with nationalism, xenophobia, and protectionism (see e.g., Perrineau 1997). Moreover, it has also been claimed that the very experience of a referendum can ease the progress of RRP parties. This is because they tend to cut across party loyalties and established political cleavages, which can aggravate political mistrust and not least weaken the bonds between the voters and the mainstream parties (Goul Andersen & Bjørklund 1990; 2000: 194). The Danish and Norwegian progress parties both emerged in 1973, close on the heels of the referenda on joining the EU. No such referendum was held in Sweden since the country had not applied for membership, which Andersen & Bjørklund see as part of the reason for why no Swedish counterpart to such parties appeared during the 1970s (cf. chapter 3). Since then, there have been referenda in Sweden in both the 1980s (on nuclear power) and 1990s (on joining the EU). The Green Party was founded as a result of the nuclear power campaign, and won parliamentary seats in 1988, which seems to corroborate Andersen & Bjørklund's hypothesis. Yet the referendum on the EU in 1994 has not had the same effect. Why is that?

I contend that there are four, partly related, main reasons for this. First, an alternative political dimension, which overlapped with a populist dimension, had already been established in Sweden. Second, issues such as immigration and national identity were toned down in the election campaign that preceded the referendum. Third, the campaign in itself was relatively modest and toned down. Finally, and partly as a result of the first three factors, other parties (especially the Left Party and the Greens, as well as the Center Party) were able to mobilize most of the EU skeptic vote.

According to Oscarsson (1996), alternative cleavage dimensions emerged in response to the priority given to nuclear power (1970s), the environment (1980s), and the EU (1990s) in the political debate. These cleavage dimensions had a number of features in common. For example, they gathered the Left, Green, and Center parties onto the same side of the cleavage, across the line from the Social Democrat, the Conservative, and the Liberal parties. The former group was opposed to nuclear power and the EU, and has traditionally been perceived as favoring the environment over economic growth. The latter group adopted the opposite stance. The Green Party, however, was not around until the 1980s, while the pro-nuclear, pro-EU group should also include the Christian Democrats, which won parliamentary representation in 1991. There were also ideological similarities between these three different cleavage dimensions. All pitted small-scale production against mass production, and the centralization of production, power, and decision-making against their decentralization. To take things to the extreme, we could say that inherent to these cleavage dimensions was a fear of change and novelty and a sense of insurgency against the political establishment (Oscarsson 1996: 246). These aspects also characterize populism, which means that there was a nascent populist cleavage dimension in Sweden at the time. The fact that established political parties have appeared with their roots deeply embedded in this niche has, however, stunted the political potential of new populist parties.

This highlights the importance of timing for social as well as political processes. The order in which events occur is crucial, as representatives of the historical-institutional school have claimed (see, e.g., Steinmo et al. 1992). In Sweden, the traditional socioeconomic right-left dimension was challenged by the nuclear issue (even if this was in a way anticipated by the student movement, and related movements, during the last years of the 1960s), which made way for the creation of a new, alternative cleavage dimension. This, in turn, shaped party positions and voter orientations on issues that were to enter center stage at a later date.

Second, issues that could be related to xenophobia and nationalism were of little relevance to the EU referendum campaign. We can also observe that although immigrant/immigration-skeptic voters were, not surprisingly, more inclined to vote against EU accession, this correlation was weak. Nor did nationalism have any strong impact on how people placed their votes (Oscarsson 1996: 254–255).

Third, the referendum campaign was relatively toned down and avoided any major subversive controversies. In fact it was calmer and more modest than a pre-general election campaign, and involved no large-scale organized manifestations designed to mobilize the voters one way or the other; there were only a handful of public meetings, fewer posters than in a general election, and practically no major TV debates. And, not least, there were uncommonly few controversial remarks from leading politicians and other opinion builders (Esaiasson 1996: 35). We could thus venture that the Swedish referendum on EU membership did not challenge established party cleavages as dramatically as in many other Western European countries; nor did it result in dissolution of established party loyalties to the same extent. One indication of the subdued mood of the referendum is that only 37 percent of the voters were able, when asked, to indicate the position (either for or against the EU) of all seven parliamentary parties. Compare this to the nuclear power referendum in 1980, when such a task was not beyond the capabilities of 66 percent of the voters (Oscarsson 1996: 239).

Fourth, and partly as a result of the above three factors, the Green and Left parties were able to attract most EU-skeptic voters. Only 9 percent of Green Party voters advocated Swedish membership, while 82 percent were opposed. Similarly, only 10 percent of the Left Party voters were in favor of joining, as opposed to 79 percent against (Lindahl 1997: 165). This is logical given that the voters perceived these two parties as the most EU-skeptic. When invited to place the parties on a scale from 0 (firmly opposed to the EU) to 10 (strongly in favor of the EU), the Greens scored an average of 1.1, the Left Party 1.6, the Center Party 5.3, the Christian Democrats 6.3, the Liberal Party 7.1, and the Conservative Party 9.4 (Oscarsson 1996: 244). The Green and Left parties also increased their support in the polls in connection with the EU referendum, from 3 to 12 percent and 4 to 13 percent respectively between 1993 and 1995 (Statistics Sweden 2002). Since then, however, support for both parties has receded.

In sum, then, we can see that the Swedish referendum on EU membership did not help to create favorable conditions for the emergence of an electorally successful Swedish RRP party. The consequences of the 2003 EMU referendum, whose campaigns were waged in an occasionally harsh ideological and political climate, remain to be seen. On the other hand, the Sweden Democrats failed to fully exploit the EMU referendum to disseminate its own political message. EU opposition still lives, and may still become politicized at some point in the future. Yet even if there was a niche for a new EU-skeptical party—as many voters who oppose the EU did not share the Green and Left parties' views on other policies or their fundamental values—this potential niche largely disappeared in 2004 when a new EU-skeptical party, the June List, emerged and gathered 14.4 percent of the votes in the June election to the European Parliament. The June List tried hard to profile itself as being beyond established party cleavages and that every second of its candidates should be left leaning and every second right leaning. There is currently an ongoing discussion that the June List might try to transform itself into a national party running in the general election of 2006. In any case, the emergence of the June List most likely resulted in shrinking niches for the Sweden Democrats or any other Swedish RRP party hoping to mobilize voters on an EU-skeptical message.

Convergence in the Swedish party space?

As mentioned in chapter 2, the degree of convergence in political space is important for three reasons. Firs, it can create the impression that the mainstream parties "are all the same," that is to say, exhibit no real, tangible differences. This, in turn, can aggravate the popular distrust of politicians and make the voters more receptive to the RRP parties' message that the "political class" is degenerate and unrepresentative of the people's interests. Second, convergence can also have a direct impact. If, in line with the spatial theory, we assume that voters opt for the party closest to their own position in political space, convergence leads to the emergence of niches within which a new party can situate itself in order to attract voters (Down 1957; Sjöblom 1968). Third, a convergence in the dominant cleavage dimension can help to depoliticize the dominant socioeconomic dimension and elevate alternative cleavage dimensions, such as the sociocultural cleavage dimension.

It is therefore worth pointing out, in respect of this study, that Swedish political space has seen no major convergence over the past decade. When asked to place the parties on a right-left scale (where 0 represented the far left and 10 the far right), voters gave the Conservative Party a score of 8.9 in the 1979 and 1982 elections, 9.0 in 1985, 8.9 again in 1988, 8.7 in 1991, 8.8 in 1994, and 8.9 once more in the election of 1998. Similarly, the Left Party was consistently placed between 0.9 and 1.4 between 1979 and 1998. The Social Democrats, however, as we found in preceding chapters, have migrated to the right since the mid 1980s (with the exception of the 1994 election) and between 1994 and 1998 drifted from 3.2 to 3.8 (Holmberg 2000: 124). Having said this, this method tells us nothing about how the voters actually interpret the terms "left" and "right," and we can suppose that they very much base their distinction on the parties' respective positions on the economic scale. At the same time, however, we know that the sociocultural dimension (which involves issues of nationality and nationalism, immigration, abortion, law, security, and so on) is more fundamental to the emergence of RRP parties (Rydgren 2003b). Accordingly, going by the above polls, we cannot categorically dismiss the possible presence, now or in the past, of a convergence as regards the sociocultural dimension.

And there are tentative indications that this might be the case (or at least was around the time of the 1998 election). When the voters were asked about their attitudes to "the multicultural society" and invited to place themselves on a scale from 0 (strongly disapprove) to 100 (strongly approve), Conservative Party voters scored an average of 58, Center Party voters 59, Social Democrat voters 60, Christian Democrat voters 61, Left Party voters 65, Green Party voters 71, and Liberal Party voters 73 (Holmberg 2000: 134). This suggests that a vacant niche might exist for voters who are opposed to the concept of the multicultural society, although we should not forget that the sociocultural cleavage dimension has played a subordinate role for the Swedish voters' choice of party (cf. Oscarsson 1998).

The relationship with established political actors

Unlike many other Western European countries (such as Denmark and France), the mainstream parties in Sweden have effectively erected a *cordon sanitaire* against the Sweden Democrats, avoiding any kind of collaboration and any anti-immigrant rhetoric; nor have they explicitly tried to appropriate the political program of this or any other anti-immigrant party.

Despite this, there have been occasions when the mainstream parties, by suggesting a more restrictive asylum and immigration policy, have migrated toward the RRP camp in this area. Take the more austere immigration and asylum line adopted by the Social Democrat government after 1994, for example. Leif Blomberg, former leader of the metal workers' union, was generally considered a "hawk" and his appointment as minister with responsibility for immigration brief after the general election of 1994 emitted clear signals that the Government was shifting ground toward stricter immigration policy. In 1996, it tightened up legislation by removing certain legal grounds of asylum, such as conscientious objection, and the term "*de facto* refugee" was also removed.

These moves were heavily criticized by other parties, especially the Left, Green, and Liberal parties, who censured the Social Democrats for effectively implementing New Democracy's asylum policy proposals in (for instance) invoking a more exclusive interpretation of the term "political refugee" (see Widfeldt 2004). Be that as it may, the fact remains that the Social Democrats, in making such legislative amendments, limited any new party's prospects of scoring political points with a similar rhetoric to that plied by New Democracy. At the same time, however, they risked subsequently legitimizing New Democracy and the policies it propagated. However, in that there was no credible (radical) right-wing populist contender at the time, there was nobody there to exploit any legitimizing effect, which is probably why this helped to constrict the political opportunity structures for new (radical) right-wing populist parties. Meanwhile the Social Democrats have become more vociferous proponents (at least discursively) of the multicultural society, which has no doubt obscured somewhat the impression of their more restrictive asylum and immigration line.

Another example of this occasional flirtation with (radical) right-wing populism is the proposals by the Liberal Party for making citizenship more conditional. The 2002 election campaign thus introduced the idea of Swedish language and history tests for immigrants, a demand that the Sweden Democrats had long had on their political agenda, albeit in a much more radical form. All this placed immigration center stage in the election campaign, although it must be stressed here that the Liberal Party did not adopt the Sweden Democrats' rhetoric and phraseology.

To take a further example, in January 2004 two leading politicians in Malmö (Social Democrat Ilmar Reepalu and Thorbjörn Lindqvist of the Conservative Party) proposed a five-year moratorium on immigration for unemployed foreign nationals wanting to settle in Malmö (including those with residence permits), winning the commendation of the Sweden Democrats in the process.

It should be remembered, however, that there is a general consensus to avoid all collaboration and coalitions with the Sweden Democrats. This has largely been observed, even in municipalities where one or another of the political blocs would have gained from cutting political deals with local Sweden Democrats politicians.

The *cordon sanitaire* erected by the mainstream parties has had a profound impact on the lack of progress made by the Sweden Democrats on the national electoral arena. In a situation where the mainstream parties appropriate the messages and rhetoric of the RRP parties, the saliency of immigration as a political issue can increase markedly, as we could partly see after the Liberal Party's language test proposal during the 2002 election campaign. Such an occurrence also helps to legitimize RRP parties, facilitating as it does their ambitions for creating and/or maintaining a sufficiently respectable façade (Rydgren 2003a). Such an opportunity was denied the Sweden Democrats, a party desperately in need of greater political respectability.

The media also has a central role to play in this context. An emerging RRP party and the political platform it represents are often "sensational" and, being therefore of considerable journalistic interest, can attract greater press coverage than they would otherwise warrant. Such tendencies have been discernible in the Swedish media, albeit muted in comparison with most other European countries, since Le Pen's gains in the French presidential election in the spring of 2002 (when, e.g., the Liberal leader Lars Lejonborg's decision to conduct a televised debate with the Sweden Democrats gave the Swedish RRP party media attention). Unlike, for instance, Denmark (see Rydgren 2004a), the Swedish media have, with a few exceptions (such as when the tabloid *Expressen* commissioned a debate article from the Sweden Democrats to publish during the EMU campaign) refrained from publishing debate articles and letters penned by the Sweden Democrats, as well as advertisements for the party. So the actions of the press also contributed on the whole to curb the Sweden Democrats' powers of voter mobilization.

The Sweden Democrats: ethnonationalism, xenophobia, and dissent

The Sweden Democrats, Sweden's leading RRP party, was formed in 1988 as a direct successor of the Sweden Party, which in turn was the outcome of a merger in 1986 of the Swedish Progress Party and the BBS (Keep Sweden Swedish) (Larsson & Ekman 2002; Lodenius & Larsson 1994; Lodenius & Wikström 1997). The Sweden Democrats has its roots in Swedish fascism, and there were, particularly at the end of the 1980s and for the first half of the 1990s, distinct overlaps between them and openly antidemocratic, Nazi, and fascist groupings (Larsson & Ekman 2001). During the latter half of the 1990s, however, the party worked hard to erect a more respectable façade. A uniform ban was introduced in 1996 by new leader Mikael Jansson (previously active in the Center Party) and in 1999 the Sweden Democrats openly renounced Nazism. Furthermore, some of the more provocative paragraphs in the party manifesto were also toned down or eventually deleted (in particular those dealing with capital punishment, the banning of abortion, and non-European adoption, to which the party was strongly opposed).

However, and notwithstanding the remarkable continuity to the party manifesto over the years up to 2002, this softer profile precipitated a split in the summer of 2001 when a disgruntled "traditionalist" faction (including Anders Steen and Tor Paulsson) broke away to form the National Democrats.

When reading the Sweden Democrats' manifesto and its political rhetoric in general, we find that the party has clearly become increasingly influenced by the electoral successes of other European RRP parties. While the British National Front was one of the larger sources of inspiration during the latter half of the 1980s, its French Front National made a profound impression on the ideological and strategic direction taken by the Sweden Democrats during the 1990s along with, albeit to a lesser extent, the Austrian FPÖ, the Danish People's Party, the German Die Republikaner, and Italy's Alleanza Nationale. For example, the leader of Die Republikaner, Franz Schönhuber, once appeared as a guest speaker at the Sweden Democrats' election meetings, and the French Front National made substantial contributions to the party's 1998 election campaign fund. The party logo, the Swedish flag as a burning torch, is a direct derivation of the British National Front's emblem and very close to that of the Front National's and Italy's neofascist MSI party. The party has also made explicit its desire to work more closely with other RRP parties (Johansson 2002: 5).

Like most of these parties, the Sweden Democrats is a pronounced culturalist party, whose program is based on ethnopluralist nationalism and xenophobia. It also accords with other RRP parties in making frequent use of the antiestablishment strategy.

To quote from the party's 2002 manifesto (which is partly a revised version of the 1990 one), "The Sweden Democrats' primary political goal is to defend our national identity" (Sverigedemokraterna 2002). This ambition rests upon an ontological relationship to the terms "people" and "culture" (i.e., to the notion that each nation embodies *one* ethnically determined culture) and a nostalgic belief in what I have previously called "the myth of the golden past" (Rydgren 2003b), a yearning for an imagined *gemeinschaft* free of conflict and social problems. This pillar of Sweden Democrats' ideological message is manifest from the party's statement of principles, which it published in 2003:

> The critical ingredient of a safe, harmonic, solid and supportive society is the common identity, which in turn requires a high degree of ethnic and cultural uniformity amongst the people. From this, it follows that the nationalist principle, the principle of one state, one nation, is absolutely fundamental to the Sweden Democrats' political values. The nationalist principle is based on the concept of the nation state, that the territorial boundaries of the state

shall coincide with its demographic boundaries. In its ideal form, such a society is therefore ethnically homogenous. . . . Cultural diversity is as necessary to mankind as biological diversity is to nature. The different cultures are mankind's common heritage and they should be acknowledged and kept apart for the benefit of us all. . . . Countries containing a multiple of relatively strong cultures have tended to develop in such a way that they end up diluting the different ethnicities and totally eradicating their original identities. We the Sweden Democrats believe that the safest way to protect the diversity of cultures, taking into consideration respect for human rights, is to do so as much as possible in the paradigm of the nation state. (Sverigedemokraterna 2003)

This philosophy thus treats cultures as unique, yet fragile, and when different cultures come together in one and the same state, the integrity of the unique, dominant national identity is jeopardized. Consequently, the Sweden Democrats, in accordance with other RRP parties, advocate ethnic segregation. In the words of party secretary Torbjörn Kastell (2002: 13), the party wants "a multicultural world, not a multicultural society."

According to the Sweden Democrats, immigration, supranationality (e.g., the EU), cultural imperialism (mainly from the U.S.A.) and globalization (they also want a check on economic globalism) were the greatest threats to the unique Swedish culture, to "Swedishness"; and by far their greatest concern was immigration. For according to the party:

The tendency in modern times has been towards incredibly widespread immigration from distant countries. An explicit goal to create a pluralistic society has seriously jeopardized the Swedish nation and its homogenous composition. There can be no doubt that such a policy constitutes a grave violation of the nationalist principle (Sverigedemokraterna 2003). . . . The mass immigration of the past decades has come to pose a serious threat to our national identity by creating huge areas populated by people who will never see themselves as Swedish nor as part of our culture or our history. Thanks to an irresponsible immigration policy designed to create a "multicultural society," new ethnic minorities have established themselves on Swedish soil, with growing social problems being the result (Sverigedemokraterna 2002).

Consequently, the Sweden Democrats advocates a highly restrictive immigration policy that denies access to effectively all non-Europeans and imposes a citizenship condition of ten years' residency and knowledge of Swedish language and history. The party believes that "Swedish citizenship shall be a privilege for Swedes," and that not even immigrants who have acquired it are "real" Swedes, as it can "take several generations" to "become fully part of a nation" (Sverigedemokraterna 2003). Today, however, the Sweden Democrats' official line is that immigrants who have already obtained citizenship shall be assimilated (i.e., shall fully renounce their "old" culture and customs—including religious beliefs if they are Muslims). The demand for a retroactive repatriation of immigrants was abandoned in 1999 when the manifesto was revised; prior to this, however, the party explicitly pursued a policy of repatriation, as this speech by party leader Mikael Jansson from a propaganda video in 1996 illustrates:

> We are not for some kind of voluntary return; we are demanding the repatriation of these people, the ones who've come here as refugees from foreign cultures since 1970. We are not talking about Western and Nordic citizens or Northwest European citizens. It's not that type of immigration that has been going on for centuries, *that* we can handle. But we cannot handle immigration from distant and culturally remote places. We simply cannot handle it (quoted from Larsson & Ekman 2001: 166).

Regardless of this change, which should be seen in light of the necessity of improving the Sweden Democrats' respectability, the party's ideological and strategic core is to claim the "Swedish people's right" to Sweden: "Sweden is the country of the Swedes. In saying this the Sweden Democrats are not saying that we Swedes are better than others, just that Sweden is the only place on earth where we have an inalienable right to live and work and develop our own individuality and identity. . . . Let Sweden remain Swedish" (Sverigedemokraterna 2003). In defining "Swedish" as "a person other Swedes see as being Swedish" (Sverigedemokraterna 2002), they are excluding all immigrants with a different appearance (not only culturally determined but also biologically, such as hair and skin color) from the Swedish national community. Given that such a definition risks excluding, in effect, all second or third generation immigrants who are fully integrated, the Sweden Democrats have accordingly embedded into their political message not only cultural racism but biological racism as well. And although the party, as already mentioned, has abandoned its demand for a retroactive forced repatriation of immigrants, they still hope to indirectly prevail upon Swedes with immigrant backgrounds to leave the country. Take the following remarks by Torbjörn Kastell made in an interview with journalist Mustafa Can:

> We will not forcibly deport immigrants and refugees—they will move of their own accord since we will make it unappealing for them to live in Sweden. We will do away with all integration projects and "cute" intercultural mingling between Swedes and immigrants. Healthcare and jobs will go to Swedes first. There will be no mother tongue teaching. No special food in schools. No days off for pupils and others who, say, want to celebrate their religious and cultural ceremonies. We will also forbid headscarves at the workplace and out in the streets and refuse planning permission for ethnic community centers or religious buildings. Mosques etc. shall be torn down. . . . Perhaps we could keep a mosque as a symbol of an historical era to remind future generations of a regrettable time when politicians tried to build a multicultural society (Can 2002: 10).

When Can, himself from an immigrant family, asked, "But what if my children and I still did not want to leave Sweden?" Kastell was explicit in his rejoinder: "You will. No immigrant would want to live in a society that I have just described to you" (Can 2002: 10).

As with other RRP parties, the Sweden Democrats' discourse on immigration and immigrants is constructed around four separate themes: first, as we saw above, immigration is considered a threat to Swedish culture and national identity. Second, immigration is considered the root of crime, particularly of the violent and sexual category. Consider the following declaration that appeared on party stickers distributed in 1996: "Drugs . . . Violence . . . AIDS . . . Crime . . . Immigration . . . Do *you* like living in the multicultural society?" Moreover, the Sweden Democrats' official journal SD-kuriren's website regularly published accounts of crimes committed by people with immigrant backgrounds in an attempt to create an image of immigrants being the main cause of criminality. "Armed Turk robs post office in Blackeberg" (1 February 2002) read one of the countless headlines; "Kosovo-Albanian convicted of rape—again" (2 April 2001), "Immigrants behind sexual assault in Gävle" (7 March 2002), "Iraqis in arson attempt on police station in Rosengård" (1 May 2003), "Cultural enricher arrested for shooting in Göteborg" (8 July 2001) were others. In that, for obvious reasons, no list is ever published of immigrants who *do not* commit criminal acts (which would make a cumbersomely long list) nor of the crimes committed by Swedes without an immigrant background, such a strategy can convince potential voters that the association between immigration and crime in Sweden is one of irrefutable and inevitable causality.

Incidentally, the term "cultural enricher" in the headline just mentioned is an example of what is commonly referred to as "frame transformation" (Benford & Snow 2000), whereby a group attempts to destroy its political opponent's central concepts by redefining them and imbuing them with new connotations. Thus in this case "cultural enricher," a term originally coined to denote the way immigrants can influence the community by providing fresh cultural stimulation, is applied in a pejorative context. Another relevant example of frame transformation is the way immigrants, as opposed to the Swedish "nationalists," are accused of being the actual racists. Torbjörn Kastell illustrates this discursive strategy thus: "These loathsome gang rapes are committed by men with immigrant backgrounds who single out Swedish women to be their victims. This is racism. The muggings committed by immigrant gangs are also exclusively against Swedish victims. This is racism." It is also interesting that the focus is on sex crimes. An election poster from 1998 announced, for example, "Tonight yet another Swedish woman will be raped. Women reclaim your freedom! Vote Swedish!" One of the Sweden Democrats' more successful campaigns, in the sense of the attention it generated, was a leafleting drive it launched in schools after a gang rape in the Stockholm suburbia Rissne "exposing" the immigrant backgrounds of the suspects and the allegedly racial motive behind the assault, as immigrants think it "not as wrong to rape a Swedish girl." Party member Kenneth Sandberg even went as far as to claim that immigration to Sweden is in danger of sparking off a civil war:

> It is never easy to make any definite statements about timetables, but I feel without a doubt that four more years of the same immigration policy and we will end up with something not unlike a civil war. . . . It is becoming more and more common to hear about four dark-skinned youths robbing and attacking defenseless old people on their way home from the post office with their meager pensions. And our young boys, blonde, blue-eyed, are being humiliated and robbed of their mobile phones. A completely new phenomenon in Swedish history is the group rape of our girls (interview in Can 2002: 11).

Third and fourth, immigration is seen as a cause of unemployment and of the financial constraints and problems of the welfare state. Immigrants are generally depicted as illegitimate competition for scant resources, which in the rhetoric of the Sweden Democrats should fall to "ethnic Swedes." Like the French Front National, the Sweden Democrats have promulgated the principle of "the national preference," by which is meant that "Swedes" are to be given priority access to child care, jobs, and health care, all under the motto, "Swedes first!," a highly potent slogan that plays on jealousy and that singles out a convenient scapegoat for the problems faced by many people in their everyday lives. Further examples from the SD-Kuriren website that trumpet out this theme include "Immigrants in the fast lane," in which immigrants are blamed for the housing crisis. Immigrants are often pitted against pensioners in the party's political propaganda, like in this election leaflet from 1998: "Greater relief for Sweden's pensioners. . . . Stop mass immigration." Here too the party has used frame transformation as a discursive strategy by repeatedly claiming that it is in fact Swedes who are the victims of discrimination. Proposals or speeches on labor market quotas are one common tactic, such as in this comment by Kastell: "[Social Democratic Minister of Integration] Mona Sahlin, one of our top politicians, has said that if two people with similar qualifications apply for the same job, it should go to the one called Mohammed. This is racism" (Kastell 2001: 2). The idea that immigrants are discriminated against (Rydgren 2004c) is, however, dismissed by the party as a falsehood.

The Sweden Democrats also adopt sociocultural right-wing authoritarian positions on issues related to family policy and law and order. Like other RRP parties, the Sweden Democrats consider the family as the most fundamental unit of society besides that of the nation, and are horrified over what they see as today's "moral disintegration," represented, for example, by divorce and abortion. Yet it is in this area where we find the greatest changes taking place over time. Since the release of the party's first manifesto in 1989, capital punishment and an abortion ban have been struck from their list of demands (with effect from the late 1990s) even though an internal debate on these issues is still raging. The deletion of these demands and the more toned-down posture together represent an attempt by the party to erect the respectable façade it needs to forestall voter alienation.

However, the party's economic policy is fairly uncontroversial, and in this sense the term "center party," which the party uses to profile itself, is not wholly misleading. This becomes apparent when we look at the areas for which, according to Johan Rinderheim (2001: 12), member of the party executive, the state should have primary responsibility: "National and local government should look after defense, both civil and military; policing and law; economic defense; fire fighting and the blue light services; overall national communication, including lighthouses and shipping lane markers; healthcare, including the prevention of infection; schools and education; internal administration." As we can thus see, the Sweden Democrats, like most other contemporary RRP parties but unlike New Democracy, do not expound a neoliberal philosophy, as the state is given an important role in the economy. It should, however, be remembered that the party's economic policy is not given much prominence and is subordinate to its ethnopluralistic ideology.

We find that the Sweden Democrats are populist mainly through their use of the antiestablishment strategy: all other political parties are lumped together into one political class, and any significant differences separating them are rarely acknowledged (even if the left—in the broad sense—is archenemy number one). Party member Jimmy Windeskog (1999: 8f) counts, for example, all political opponents, including the mainstream parties, as part of the "liberal-Marxist establishment." The reason for this label is apparently "the fact that socialism/Marxism and liberalism have converged and are today in the same boat heading towards a genderless, egalitarian, multicultural utopia. . . . The liberal-Marxist establishment comprises two different kinds of people: those who have no grasp of reality and those who *pretend* not to have a grasp of reality." This is, then, what the Sweden Democrats place themselves in opposition to, posing as the party that not only has witnessed reality but that also has the courage to describe it. Like the French Front National, the Sweden Democrats crow about "saying what common people think, and saying it loud" (cf. Larsson & Ekman 2001: 277) instead of keeping to the politically correct. In that the Sweden Democrats consider demographic (ethnic) homogeneity as a necessary condition of a peaceful and functional democratic society, all the mainstream parties (that in one way or another favor immigration and asylum) are seen as the grave-diggers of democracy. So according to the party, the Sweden Democrats are not the enemies of democracy, but its greatest champion. This "political class" is also depicted as undemocratic and rooted in self-interest—the "interpreters of the public interest" (Sverigedemokraterna 2002) and "the people's true voice" being the Sweden Democrats, who are the only true democratic alternative. They also claim to be the victims of a "doctrinal dictatorship" created by a process "that gives 'approved' internationally oriented politicians leading positions in society" and by an "extremely homogenous media [and] TV and radio monopoly" (Sverigedemokraterna 2002).

However, the main obstacle facing the Sweden Democrats has been the credible use of the second component of the populist antiestablishment strategy: to not appear, in spite of its dissentious attitudes, as overly extreme or too closely associated with openly antidemocratic groups. As we have seen, the party has its roots in the extraparliamentary far right, and for the first half of the 1990s there was no clear distinction between the Sweden Democrats and different skinhead and Nazi organizations, and an overlap of membership was not uncommon (Larsson & Ekman 2001). We can see this proximity not least in light of the pressure felt by Mikael Jansson, as the newly appointed leader, to impose a uniform ban in 1996 and to repeatedly urge members not to wear uniforms at party meetings up to 1999. As we can read in the following extract from the newsletter *Jansson's bulletin*, it was, however, only the superficial symbols of political extremism that were forbidden, and this for strategic reasons: "The Sweden Democrats have earned a bad reputation because certain 'Hollywood Nazis' and other people in quasi-uniforms had joined the annual Engelbrekt March. . . . People with such weak convictions that they have to dress in a manner that bring ridicule and shame onto the Sweden Democrats we order to stay at home. . . . We will be photographing and publishing pictures of those who actively damage the party" (from *SD-Bulletinen*, March 1996; quoted in Larsson & Ekman 2001: 168f). Nevertheless, the party did not explicitly renounce Nazism until 1999/2000 after the events in the small town Malexander (when two policemen were murdered by three armed criminals with links to Nazi movements) and the murder of syndicalist Björn Söderberg, which brought the Sweden Democrats also under media scrutiny to disastrous results, publicity-wise (see Larsson & Ekman 2001: 171). In 2003, the party took a further step toward ridding itself of the stigma of extremism by announcing that the UN declaration on human rights was to form a cornerstone of its policies. Although the increased support for the Sweden Democrats in the past few years is partly due to the effectiveness of these changes, there is much to suggest that the party is still seriously hurt by its extremist image among a large portion of the electorate. Not only are these changes comparatively new (and will probably only have a full effect, if at all, in the future), there are also clear signs that not everyone has taken them to heart and that they have not been properly implemented throughout the organization (or even the party executive). A good many statements have been made that have stepped over the official "respectable" line, and since many of the party's leading members were active already during the early 1990s (such as Mikael Jansson and Johan Rinderhem), it can be hard to give a credible explanation as to why they, as confirmed democrats, chose to join an extremist party in which one in three members of the executive had Nazi links (Larsson & Ekman 2001: 165). As we will now see, there have also been voices from within the organization opposing the abandonment of old ideological principles, and this has also caused serious problems for the party.

Organization: few alternative resources and strong path-dependency

Unlike New Democracy, the Sweden Democrats have had little access to alternative resources, whether party subsidy or major private donations, and/or to the media. Consequently, the party has been heavily dependent on its members and party activists and the voluntary work they do. And unlike New Democracy, the Sweden Democrats have aspired to build a popular base, a "movement," made up of well developed local associations (which seems to be an unfinished project, as the Sweden Democrats only managed to put forward candidates in a mere 80 municipalities—of 289 in total—for the 2002 general election). Despite the fact that these ambitions could one day rescue the Sweden Democrats from the same fate that awaited New Democracy when the party lost its electoral representation, at which time it possessed no organizational infrastructure to keep the party alive (see chapter 4), it also means that the Sweden Democrats lack the advantages that New Democracy originally had to secure its electoral breakthrough. As we have seen, the Sweden

Democrats are not a newly formed party and are encumbered by the chains of a far from flattering history. This does not only frustrate the credible use of the second component of the popular antiestablishment strategy, as we saw above, it also aggravates the goal conflict between the voter and internal arenas (see chapter 2), as there are members who identify strongly with ideological principles and old manifesto tenets and objectives that are not optimal in terms of attracting electoral support (and are more likely to frighten off potential voters). This goal conflict is also exacerbated by the way in which the Sweden Democrats are so desperately dependent on party members for the peddling of their message—and for enabling the party to function in the first place. As Larsson and Ekman (2001: 212) have insightfully noted, the Sweden Democrats are facing a difficult and awkward dilemma:

> If the Sweden Democrats, on the one hand, openly appear as a "national" [i.e. proto-fascist] party in the way that it did in the first half of the 1990s, it will probably scare off its potential voters. If, on the other hand, the party continues to "liberalize" its rhetoric and tone down the opinions that make up its ideological core, it risks becoming so mediocre that key members of the activist cadre will abandon it. It is these passionate devotees to the cause and their tireless voluntary work, leafleting and public rallying that have kept the party running.

There are no clear answers to how the party will deal with this dilemma and we have seen how the executive has occasionally tried to resolve the conflict by adopting one rhetorical line externally (toward the voters) and another internally (toward the members). At critical junctures, such as when it is time to revise the party manifesto and principle program or to specify the contents of the election campaign, the conflict has flared up and triggered a wave of defections and party splits.

As Gamson (1975: 101) has written, "Factional splits . . . are the primary manifestation of the failure of the group to resolve the problem of internal conflicts." Internal conflicts there will always be, to a greater or lesser extent, but they are likely to be greater and more common in parties which, like the Sweden Democrats, (1) are marginalized (which increases the pressure on internal cohesion); (2) have a strong ideological conviction of an almost messianic nature (of having "seen the light" and of needing to "rescue society from annihilation"); and (3) sprung up as "front organizations" to unite disparate groups (which means that the party was ideologically divided already from the beginning). As a result, the party has suffered various defections, exclusions and splits. It is significant that two of the party's most recent organizers, Tor Paulsson and Tommy Funebo, have left the party under traumatic circumstances. The first instance, when Paulsson left the Sweden Democrats together with Anders Steen and several others in protest at, in their eyes, an over-liberalization of policy to form the National Democrats (which is a far more radical right-wing authoritarian and explicitly xenophobic party), might paradoxically enough have benefited the Sweden Democrats, despite its losing a substantial segment of its activists, not least at a local level. Political players can sometimes gain from what are known as "radical flank" effects (e.g., Tarrow 1998). After the appearance of the National Democrats on the voter arena, the Sweden Democrats was no longer the most extreme of extremist parties and might even appear, in comparison with their new rival, rather restrained and level-headed. This possibly helped to reduce the party's stigma and enabled it to make more credible use of the populist antiestablishment strategy.

On the other hand, it is likely that the latest loss, that of Tommy Funebo and a number of leading local party politicians, all of whom joined the SPI (a pensioners' party), will seriously damage the party. This time it was the defectors who (with a certain measure of authority) accused the party of using far-right and undemocratic methods rather than vice versa. The executive moved to dispel the rumors of a split. According to an article by party member Mattias Karlsson in the party newsletter, the latest conflicts were caused by the party's deliberate drive to recruit new activists to be able to participate in local elections in as many municipalities as possible:

> The obvious advantages of this strategy were that it gave us more seats, more electoral support, more money and more publicity, which all in all also greatly improved our chances of getting into parliament after the 2006 election. At the same time, a number of skilled activists and competent politicians have been recruited into the party, some of whom might have been disheartened if they had not been allowed to stand in their home constituencies. The only possible downside of this way of doing things is that the party found itself no longer able to keep as close tabs on each candidate as it has done on previous elections, when we just had candidates in a handful of places. . . . It does not matter how fine the net, there are always a few rotten fish that slip through, and that's been the case here too (*SD Newsletter*, 13 January 2004).

Representatives of the party's inner circle, Mikael Jansson, Björn Söder, and Johan Rinderheim, gave a similar explanation:

> As a growing party we must constantly go through a process of cleansing to separate the wheat from the chaff. Put bluntly, this means that a party in its formation stage always attracts a number of individuals with everything but the party's and the country's best at heart. Such unsuitable people must of course be sidelined and removed, if it does not happen naturally. In some cases this entails a temporary loss for the party but in the long run such a purging process is necessary if we are one day to have a genuine influence on Swedish politics (*SD Newsletter*, 13 January 2004).

However, this is only partly true (some expulsions have been made for racist remarks or criminal activity, while a number of defections have occurred for different reasons), and is clearly a deliberate attempt to legitimize the party by delegitimizing its defectors. Nevertheless, it is a perfect illustration of the Sweden Democrats' problems: to create a working national party organization, to resolve the goal conflict between the voter and internal arenas, and, most importantly of all, to apply the populist antiestablishment strategy credibly. The fact that the party is still perceived as far too extremist expels voters and is one of the most important reasons for why the party has not managed to exploit potential niches and other political opportunity structures for voter mobilization. There is, in spite of everything, a potential for continued growth on the voter arena for the party; even though in 2003 only 3 percent of the voters more or less approved of the Sweden Democrats, 7 percent answered "neither like nor dislike" to the question of what they thought about the party (FSI, 2003). It is in this latter group where the party's potential resides.

Conclusion

This chapter has discussed a number of factors that have obstructed the growth of an electorally successful Swedish RRP party. First, we have seen indicators that there is still a considerable measure of class awareness and class loyalty in Sweden. This is significant as it suggests that established collective identities and loyalties have not been eroded in Sweden to the same extent as in other European countries. It also indicates that the socioeconomic cleavage dimension is still of relatively high salience for the Swedish voters—something that is also shown by the way that political issues belonging to this dimension have continued to dominated their agenda throughout this past decade—which reduces the chances of a new party winning votes by promoting sociocultural politics.

Second, immigration has been of relatively little concern to the Swedish electorate. Although many have seen it as an important issue, it has had little impact on their choice of party. In Sweden, the economic crisis and the high rate of unemployment that came in its wake led to a shift toward the left along the economic cleavage dimension rather than to increased salience of authoritarianism and xenophobia. Third, the degree of convergence in political space has been only slight in Sweden. The Conservative Party have been consistently thought the only real right-wing alternative, which has contradicted the notion of there being no real difference between the mainstream parties and impeded a depoliticization of the socioeconomic cleavage dimension.

We have, however, also found traces of a potential niche within which the Sweden Democrats or some other Swedish RRP party would be able to build up strength in the near future. There is in Sweden, as elsewhere, a widespread mood of popular xenophobia and hostility toward immigrants; although this is not as strong as it was in the early 1990s, immigration became once again a central issue of the 2002 election campaign. Moreover, people's confidence in politicians, parties, and other political institutions is about as low in Sweden as in other countries, which can provide fertile ground for the propagation of parties both willing and able to mobilize protest votes. On top of this, the proportion of voters identifying with one or other party has declined, which has freed up resources for new political parties, while the degree of voter abstention has risen, particularly among the unemployed and working class, groups that in other Western European countries have been overrepresented among RRP supporters.

Even though the potential conditions that exist for the development of an electorally successful RRP party were greater during the economic crisis of the mid 1990s, they still exist. The absence of any such national RRP party has, I believe, at least as much to do with the supply side of politics. The Sweden Democrats have been the leading RRP party since New Democracy's breakdown in 1994. However, they have found it difficult to create for themselves a sufficiently respectable façade and to convince the voters that while they are opposed to the mainstream parties, they are not for that reason antidemocratic per se. Put another way, the Sverigedemokraterna have failed with the "anti establishment strategy." The party has also faced difficulties promulgating its political message, and visibility (not least in the media) is one condition of successful voter mobilization.

Notes

1. This does not apply, however, to the opportunities for mobilizing discontent with the EU and its institutions.

Afterword

What have we learned from this study on Swedish right-wing populism? An initial answer would be that we have learned to be skeptical of deterministic explanations of political change: even though the conditions have occasionally been favorable for the emergence of a popularly successful RRP party in Sweden, all have failed. This demonstrates the complex interplay of the factors that have to coincide for new parties to become established, such as the presence of a favorable opportunity structure and a political profile suited to exploiting it; an ability to broadcast a political message; the necessary resources; and an organization able to deal with inner conflict. In only one case has a right-wing populist party in Sweden achieved an electoral breakthrough, namely New Democracy in 1991, but it lacked the organizational buoyancy to keep the party organizations together when it met internal conflicts.

If we look back at the different political opportunity structures that we introduced in chapter 2, we can see there have been a number of factors that have told against the emergence of a Swedish (radical) right-wing populist party: (1) Crucially, the dominant socioeconomic cleavage dimension is still strong in Sweden. The key issues (for politicians, the electorate, and the media) remain pivoted upon the role of the state in the economy, something that has never failed to engage people's minds. On the other hand, the sociocultural cleavage dimension has been relatively toned down in Swedish politics, which has rendered a (radical) right-wing voter mobilization more difficult. In that the mainstream parties are still comparatively dispersed across the socioeconomic dimension, it is very hard for new parties to locate vacant niches there. An important exception was New Democracy, which benefited from a socio-economic shift to the right and which was able to outbid the neoliberal policies peddled by the Conservative Party. However, this opening lasted only a few years and was eliminated by the economic crisis of the early 1990s. (2) The lack of convergence in political space has also therefore been an impediment to embryonic (radical) right-wing populist parties. The fact that there has also been a certain degree of convergence on the rival sociocultural dimension is of little concern given the relative low salience of this dimension (even though the Left Party and, to a certain extent, the Green Party might very well have benefited from a "cultural liberal" niche along its axis).

Nevertheless, we have also identified some of the political opportunity structures that have the capacity to favor the emergence of a popularly successful Swedish (emerging) right-wing populist party: as in many other countries, (1) political trust is at a low level in Sweden, party iden-tification has waned, and the voters have become increasingly mobile; (2) there is, and has been, a significant opposition to immigration—and, to a certain extent, xenophobia—in Sweden, even if the issue has not been as dominant as in many other Western European countries.

Some factors have also changed over time. For instance, while the media was very generous in the space it gave to New Democracy ahead of the 1991 election, which lent the party vital political exposure, it has been restrictive as regards the Sweden Democrats. This is prob-ably due to the difference between the political messages and historical backgrounds of the two parties, for whereas the Sweden Democrats are a pronounced RRP party with its roots in extraparliamentary right-wing extremism, New Democracy was "only" a right-wing populist party with xenophobic overtones. This also means that the Sweden Democrats are, and have long been, more stigmatized than New Democracy—and are possibly more so than most other Western RRP parties, given the rela-tive recency of the party's extraparliamentary past.

REFERENCES

Ahrne, G. 1994. *Social Organizations: Interaction Inside, Outside and Between Organizations.* London: Sage.

Ahrne, G. and Papakostas, A. 2003. "Behövs medlemmarna?" *Sociologisk Forskning* 3/2003: 3–11.

Ahrne, G., Roman, C. and Franzén, M. 2000. *Det sociala landskapet. En sociologisk beskrivning av Sverige från 50-tal till 90-tal.* Göteborg: Bokförlaget Korpen.

Alfredsson, H.O. 1994. "Colliander lämnar politiken," *Svenska Dagbladet*, 23 June 1994.

Arter, D. 1992. "Black faces in the blond crowd: populist racialism in Scandinavia." *Parliamentary Affairs* 45(3): 357–372.

Barker, M. 1981. *The New Racism.* London: Junction.

Bell, D. 1976. *The Coming of Post-Industrial Society. A Venture in Social Forecasting.* New York: Basic Books.

Bell, D. 1996. *The Cultural Contradictions of Capitalism.* New York: Basic Books.

Benford, R.D. and Snow, D.A. 2000. "Framing processes and social movements: An overview and assessment." *Annual Review of Sociology* 26: 611–639.

Bennulf, M. 2000. "Medborgarna tycker om miljön," in Holmberg, S. and Gilljam, M. eds. *Det Nya samhället: SOM-undersökningen 1999.* Gothenburg: SOM-institutet.

Bergström, H. 1991, "Sweden's politics and party system at the crossroads." *West European Politics* 14(3): 8–30.

Berlin, I., Hofstadter, R., and MacRae, D. 1968. "To define populism." *Government and Opposition* 3: 137–179.

Betz, H-G. 1994. *Radical Right-Wing Populism in Western Europe.* London: MacMillan Press.

Betz, H-G. and Immerfall, S. 1998. eds. *The New Politics of the Right: Neo-Populist Parties and Movements in Established Democracies.* New York: St. Martin's.

Björk, R. 1994. "Bert i natt: Jag kan sluta istället." *Expressen*, 6 February 1994.

Boréus, K. 1994. *Högervåg: nyliberalismen och kampen om språket i svensk debatt 1969–1989*. Stockholm: Tiden.

Boréus, K. 1997. "The shift to the right: neo-liberalism in argumentation and language in the Swedish public debate since 1969." *European Journal of Political Research* 31(3): 257–286.

Brothén, M. 1999. "Stigande förtroende för Riksdagen under valår," in Holmberg, S. and Weibull, L. eds. *Ljusnande framtid: SOM-undersökningen 1998*. Gothenburg: SOM-institutet.

Budge, I. and Farlie, D. 1983. "Party competition—selective emphasis or direct confrontation? An alternative view with data," in Daalder, H. and Mair, P. eds. *West European Party Systems. Continuity & Change*. London: Sage.

Budge, I. and Robertson, D. 1987. "Do parties differ, and how? Comparative discriminant and factor analyses," in Budge, I., Robertson, D. and Hearl, D. eds. *Ideology, Strategy and Party Change: Spatial Analyses of Post-War Election Programmes in 19 Democracies*. Cambridge: Cambridge University Press.

Campbell, A., Converse, P.E., Miller, W.E. and Stokes, D.E. 1960. *The American Voter*. New York: John Wiley & Sons.

Can, M. 2002. "I Sveriges namn." *Dagens Nyheter* 28 September 2002.

Canovan, M. 1981. *Populism*. London: Harcourt Brace Jovanovich.

Canovan, M. 1999. "Trust the people! Populism and the two faces of democracy." *Political Studies*, XLII: 2–16.

Carlberg, P. 1991. "Missnöjespartierna vinner terräng." *Svenska Dagbladet*, 23 April 1991.

Cigéhn, G. 1990. "Klassmedvetande och klassidentifiering," in Åberg, R. ed. *Industrisamhället i omvandling*. Stockholm: Carlssons.

Cigéhn, G. 1999. "Klassidentitet vid seklets slut." *Sociologisk Forskning* 36(1).

Clark, T.N. and Lipset, S.M. 1996. "Are social classes dying?," in Lee, D.J. and Turner, B.S. eds. *Conflicts About Class. Debating Inequality in Late Industrialism*. London: Longman.

Clark, T.N. and Lipset, S.M. 2001. eds. *The Breakdown of Class Politics. A Debate on Post-Industrial Stratification*. Baltimore: The Johns Hopkins University Press.

Dahrendorf, R. 1959. *Class and Class Conflict in Industrial Society*. London: Routledge.

Dalton, R.J. 1999. "Political support in advanced industrial societies," in Norris, P. ed. *Critical Citizens. Global Support for Democratic Government*. Oxford: Oxford University Press.

Demker, M. 1993. "'Stäng gränserna!?' Svenskarnas åsikter om flyktingmottagning," in Holmberg, S. and Weibull, L. eds. *Perspektiv på krisen. SOM-undersökningen 1992*. Gothenburg: SOM-institutet.

Demker, M. 1995. "Att bli en riktig svensk," in Holmberg, S. and Weibull, L. eds. *Vägval. SOM-undersökningen 1993*. Gothenburg: SOM-institutet.

Demker, M. 2000. "Attityder till flyktingar: unga pojkar och unga flickor på var sin sida," in Holmberg, S. and Gilljam, M. eds. *Det Nya samhället: SOM-undersökningen 1999*. Gothenburg: SOM-institutet.

Demker, M. 2003. "Trendbrott i flyktingfrågan—och polariseringen har ökat," in Holmberg, S. and Weibull, L. eds. *Fåfängans marknad: SOM-undersökningen 2002.* Gothenburg: SOM-institutet.

Demker, M. and Gilljam, M. 1994. "Om rädslan för det främmande," in Holmberg, S. and Weibull, L. eds. *Vägval. SOM-undersökningen 1993.* Gothenburg: SOM-institutet.

Downs, A. 1957. *An Economic Theory of Democracy.* New York: Harper Collins Publishers.

Duverger, M. 1954. *Political Parties.* London: Methuen.

Ebbinghaus, B. and Visser, J. 2000. "A comparative profile," in Ebbinghaus, B. and Visser, J. eds. *The Societies of Europe. Trade Unions in Western Europe since 1945.* London: Macmillan.

Edgerton, D., Fryklund, B. and Peterson, T. 1994. *"Until the Lamb of God Appears . . ." The 1991 Parliamentary Election: Sweden Chooses a New Political System.* Lund: Lund University Press.

Eneberg, K. 1993. "Karlsson protesterade mot sitt parti." *Dagens Nyheter* 29 April 1993.

Epstein, L.D. 1967. *Political Parties in Western Democracies.* New Brunswick, NJ: Transaction Books.

Eriksson, G. 1994. "Nyd-val ogillas." *Svenska Dagbladet,* 2 July 1994.

Esaiasson, P. 1990. *Svenska valkampanjer 1866–1988.* Gothenburg: Allmänna förlaget.

Esaiasson, P. 1995. "Mosiga Mona och andra historier," in Holmberg, S. and Weibull, L. eds. *Vägval. SOM-undersökningen 1993.* Gothenburg: SOM-institutet.

Esaiasson, P. 1996. "Kampanj på sparlåga," in Gilljam, M. and Holmberg, S. eds. *Ett knappt ja till EU.* Stockholm: Norstedts Juridik.

Eurostat. 1996. *Eurostatistics. Data for short-term economic analysis.* European Commission. 12/1996.

Eurostat. 1999. *Statistics in focus. Population and social conditions.* European Commission. Theme 3–4/1999.

Eurostat. 2000. *Eurostatistics. Data for short-term economic analysis.* European Commission. 8–9/2000.

Falu-Kuriren. 1993. "Palatsrevolution mot Ian & Bert." 27 September 1993.

Folkbladet. 1992. "Ian & Berts fanclub." 22 February 1992.

Fryklund, B. and Peterson, T. 1981. *Populism och missnöjespartier i Norden. Studier i småborgerlig klassaktivitet.* Lund: Arkiv Förlag.

Fryklund, B. and Peterson, T. 1989. *"Vi mot dom': Det dubbla främlingskapet i Sjöbo.* Lund: Lund University Press.

FSI. 2003. "Inställningen till Sverigedemokraterna." *Forskningsgruppen för Samhälls- och Informationsstudier.* Stockholm.

Gamson, W.A. 1975. *The Strategy of Social Protest.* Homewood, Ill: The Dorsey Press.

Gardberg, A. 1993. *Against the Stranger, the Gangster and the Establishment: A Comparative Study of the Swedish Ny demokrati, the German Republikaner, the French Front National and the Belgian Vlaams Block.* Helsinki: SSKH, Helsinki University.

126   References

Gilljam, M. and Holmberg, S. 1993. *Väljarna inför 90-talet*. Stockholm: Norstedts Juridik.

Gilljam, M. and Oscarsson, H. 1994. "Svenska folkets näst bästa partier," in Holmberg, S. and Weibull, L. eds. *Vägval. SOM-undersökningen 1993*. Gothenburg: SOM-institutet.

Goffman, E. 1959. *The Presentation of Self in Everyday Life*. New York: Penguin.

Golder, M. 2003. "Explaining variations in the success of extreme right parties in Western Europe." *Comparative Political Studies* 36(4): 432–466.

Goul Andersen, J. and Bjørklund, T. 1990. "Structural changes and new cleavages: The progress parties in Denmark and Norway." *Acta Sociologica* 33(3): 195–217.

Goul Andersen, J. and Bjørklund, T. 2000. "Radical right-wing populism in Scandinavia: from tax revolt to neo-liberalism and xenophobia," in Hainsworth, P. ed. *The Politics of the Extreme Right. From the Margins to the Mainstream*. London: Pinter.

Grahnquist, K. 1991. "Sprickan ökar—hur länge skall Ian stå ut?" *Expressen*, 19 September 1991.

Granath, C. 1993. "Show i högt tempo." *Sydsvenska Dagbladet*, 1 August 1993.

Hainsworth, P. 2000. ed. *The Politics of the Extreme Right: From the Margins to the Mainstream*. London: Pinter.

Hamilton, L.C. 1998. *Statistics With Stata 5*. London: Duxbury.

Hirschman, A.O. 1970. *Exit, Voice and Loyalty: Responses to Decline in Firms, Organizations and States*. Cambridge: Harvard University Press.

Holmberg, S. 1993. "Socialdemokraterna: 'The Comback Kids,'" in Holmberg, S. and Weibull, L. eds. *Perspektiv på krisen. SOM-undersökningen 1992*. Gothenburg: SOM-institutet.

Holmberg, S. 1997. "Svenska folket är si så där nöjda med hur demokratin fungerar i Sverige," in Holmberg, S. and Weibull, L. eds. *Ett missnöjt folk? SOM-undersökningen 1996*. Gothenburg: SOM-institutet.

Holmberg, S. 2000. *Välja parti*. Stockholm: Norstedts Juridik.

Holmberg, S. and Weibull, L. 1997. "Förtroendets fall," in Holmberg, S. and Weibul, L. eds. *Ett missnöjt folk? SOM-undersökningen 1996*. Gothenburg: SOM-institutet.

Holmberg, S. and Weibull, L. 1999. "Ljusnande framtid," in Holmberg, S. and Weibull, L. eds. *Ljusnande framtid: SOM-undersökningen 1998*. Gothenburg: SOM-institutet.

Holmberg, S. and Weibull, L. 2000. "Förtroendet faller," in Holmberg, S. and Gilljam, M. eds. *Det Nya samhället: SOM-undersökningen 1999*. Gothenburg: SOM-institutet.

Holmberg, S. and Weibull, L. 2003a. "Fåfängans marknad," in Holmberg, S. and Weibull, L. eds. *Fåfängans marknad: SOM-undersökningen 2002*. Gothenburg: SOM-institutet.

Holmberg, S. and Weibull, L. 2003b. "Förgängligt förtroende," in Holmberg, S. and Weibull, L. eds. *Fåfängans marknad: SOM-undersökningen 2002*. Gothenburg: SOM-institutet.

Hout, M., Brooks, C. and Manza, J. 1996. "The persistence of classes in post-industrial societies," in Lee, D.J. and Turner, B.S. eds. *Conflicts about Class. Debating Inequality in Late Industrialism*. London: Longman.

Ignazi, P. 1996. "The crisis of parties and the rise of new political parties." *Party Politics* 2(4): 549–566.

Inglehart, R. 1997. *Modernization and Postmodernization. Cultural, Economic, and Political Change in 43 Societies*. Princeton NJ: Princeton University Press.

Johansson, G. 2002. "Partiledaren." *SD-Kuriren* 48/2002.

Jönsson, M. 1994. "Ians sorti tog Bert på sången." *Göteborgsposten*, 6 February 1994.

Karlsson, B. 1991. *Skandal!* Borås: Mariann.

Karlsson, B. 1994a. "Ian vill sänka partiet för gott." DN-debatt. *Dagens Nyheter*, 10 February 1994.

Karlsson, B. 1994b. "Jag borde ha stoppat det som pågick." DN-debatt. *Dagens Nyheter*, 17 August 1994.

Karlsson, B. and Wachtmeister, I. 1990. "Här är vårt partiprogram." DN-debatt, *Dagens Nyheter*, 25 November 1990.

Kastell, T. 2002. "Den nationalistiska grundsynen." *SD-Kuriren* 45/2002.

Kastell, T. 2001. "Sverigedemokraterna mot våld och rasism." *SD-Kuriren* 41/2001.

Katz, R.S. 1980. *A Theory of Parties and Electoral Systems*. Baltimore: Johns Hopkins University Press.

Kitschelt, H. 1994a. "Austrian and Swedish Social Democrats in crisis: party strategy and organization in corporatist regimes." *Comparative Political Studies* 27(1): 3–39.

Kitschelt, H. 1994b. *The Transformation of European Social Democracy*. Cambridge: Cambridge University Press.

Kitschelt, H. 1995. *The Radical Right in Western Europe. A Comparative Analysis*. Ann Arbor: The University of Michigan Press.

Kjellberg, A. 2000. "Sweden," in Ebbinghaus, B. and Visser, J. eds. *The Societies of Europe. Trade Unions in Western Europe since 1945*. London: Macmillan.

Klandermans, B. 1997. *The Social Psychology of Protest*. Oxford: Blackwell.

Klingemann, H-D. 1999. "Mapping political support in the 1990s: A global analysis," in Norris, P. ed. *Critical Citizens. Global Support for Democratic Government*. Oxford: Oxford University Press.

Knutsson, M. 1992. "Nyd ser chansen till ökad makt." *Svenska Dagbladet*, 11 November 1992.

Knutsson, M. 1993. "De är okunniga eller myglare." *Svenska Dagbladet*, 24 April 1993.

Kratz, A. 1992a. "Nya stadgar fråga för nyd." *Svenska Dagbladet*, 19 February 1992.

Kratz, A. 1992b. "Nyd till strid om flyktingar." *Svenska Dagbladet*, 13 July 1992.

Kriesi, H., Koopmans, R., Duyvendak, J.W. and Giugni, M.G. 1995. *New Social Movements in Western Europe. A Comparative Analysis*. Minneapolis: University of Minnesota Press.

Larsson, S. 1998. "Suède," in Camus J-Y. ed. *Les extrémismes en Europe: état des lieux en 1998*. Paris: Éditions de l'Aube.

Larsson, S. and Ekman, M. 2001. *Sverigedemokraterna. Den nationella rörelsen*. Stockholm: Ordfront /Expo.

Lawson, K. 1994. "Introduction," in Lawson, K. ed. *How Political Parties Work. Perspectives from Within*. London: Praeger.

Leijonhufvud, S. 1994. "Karlsson vill ha ett tuffare nyd." *Svenska Dagbladet*, 1 February 1994.

Lindahl, R. 1993. "Ekonomiska förhoppningar och EG-medlemskap," in Holmberg, S. and Weibull, L. eds. *Perspektiv på krisen. SOM-undersökningen 1992*. Gothenburg: SOM-institutet.

Lindahl, R. 1994. "Inför avgörandet—åsikter om EU," in Holmberg, S. and Weibull, L. eds. *Vägval. SOM-undersökningen 1993*. Gothenburg: SOM-institutet.

Lindahl, R. 1995. "Efter EU-omröstningen—svåra frågor återstår," in Holmberg, S. and Weibull, L. eds. *Vägval. SOM-undersökningen 1993*. Gothenburg: SOM-institutet.

Lindahl, R. 1997. "Missnöjda EU-medlemmar," in Holmberg, S. and Weibull, L. eds. *Ett missnöjt folk? SOM-undersökningen 1996*. Gothenburg: SOM-institutet.

Lindahl, R. 1999. "Mångtydig EU-opinion," in Holmberg, S. and Weibull, L. eds. *Ljusnande framtid: SOM-undersökningen 1998*. Göteborg: SOM-institutet.

Lipset, S.M. and Raab, E. 1970. *The Politics of Unreason. Right-wing extremism in America, 1790–1970*. New York: Harper Row.

Lipset, S.M. and Rokkan, S. 1967. "Cleavage structures, party systems, and voter alignments: an introduction," in Lipset, S.M. and Rokkan, S. eds. *Party Systems and Voter Alignments: Cross-National Perspectives*. New York: The Free Press.

Ljungaeus, D. 1992. "Ny demokrati tar till munkavle." *iDag*, 13 November 1992.

Ljungberg, D. 1993. "Tre blir utestängda från nyd." *Dagens Nyheter*, 21 August 1993.

Lodenius, A.-L. and Larsson, S. 1994. *Extremhögern*. Stockholm: Tidens förlag.

Lodenius, A.-L. and Wikström, P. 1997. *Vit makt och blågula drömmar. Rasism och nazism i dagens Sverige*. Stockholm: Natur och kultur.

MacRae, D. 1969. "Populism as an ideology," in Ionescu, G. and Gellner, E. eds. *Populism. Its Meaning and National Characteristics*. London: Weidenfeld and Nicolson.

Mair, P., Lipset, S.M., Hout, M. and Goldthorpe, J.H. 1999. "Critical commentry: Four perspective on the end of class politics?," in Evans, G. ed. *The End of Class Politics? Class Voting in Comparative Context*. New York: Oxford University Press.

Mayer, N. 1999. *Ces Français qui votent FN*. Paris: Flammarion.

McAdam, D. 1999. *Political Process and the Development of Black Insurgency, 1930–1970*. Chicago: The University of Chicago Press.

McAdam, D. and Rucht, D. 1993. "The cross-national diffusion of movement ideas." *The Annals* 528: 56–74.

McCarthy, J.D. and Zald, M.N. 1977. "Resource mobilization and social movements: a partial theory." *American Journal of Sociology* 82(6): 1212–1241.

Mellin, L. 1993. "Bert: Jag har fått nog." *Aftonbladet,* 17 March 1993.

Ménu, Y. and Surel, Y. 2000. *Par le peuple, pour le peuple. Le populisme et les démocraties.* Paris: Fayard.

Meyer, J. W. and Rowan B. 1981. "Institutionalized organizations: Formal structures as myth and ceremony," in Grusky, O. and Miller, G.A. eds. *The Sociology of Organizations. Basic Studies.* New York: Free Press.

Minkenberg, M. 1997. "The New Right in France and Germany. Nouvelle Droite, Neue Rechte, and the new right radical parties," in Merkl, P.H. and Weinberg, L. 1997. eds. *The Revival of Right-wing Extremism in the Nineties.* London: Frank Cass.

Möller, T. 2000 *Politikens meningslöshet. Om misstro, cynism och utanförskap.* Malmö: Liber.

Neiman, F. 1993. "Nu får det vara nog, Bildt!" *Aftonbladet,* 21 February 1993.

Nieuwbeerta, P. 2001. "The democratic class struggle in postwar societies: Traditional class voting in twenty countries, 1945–1990," in Clark, T.N. and Lipset, S.M. eds. *The Breakdown of Class Politics: A Debate on Post-Industrial Stratification.* Baltimore: The Johns Hopkins University Press.

Nilsson, L. 1992. "Den offentliga sektorn under åtstramning och omprövning," in Holmberg, S. and Weibull, L. eds. Trendbrott? SOM-undersökningen 1991. Gothenburg: SOM-institutet.

Nilsson, L. 1994. "Offentligt eller privat?," in Holmberg, S. and Weibull, L. eds. *Vägval. SOM-undersökningen 1993.* Gothenburg: SOM-institutet.

Nilsson, L. 1995. "Att spara eller inte spara?," in Holmberg, S. and Weibull, L. eds. *Vägval. SOM-undersökningen 1993.* Gothenburg: SOM-institutet.

Nilsson, L. 1997. "Är svenskarna lyckliga?," in Holmberg, S. and Weibull, L. eds. *Ett missnöjt folk? SOM-undersökningen 1996.* Gothenburg: SOM-institutet.

Nilsson, L. 1998. "Opinionstrender och medieeffekter," in Holmberg, S. and Weibull, L. eds. *Opinionssamhället: SOM-undersökningen 1997.* Gothenburg: SOM-institutet.

Nilsson, L. 2003. "Välfärdspolitik och legitimitet," in Holmberg, S. and Weibull, L. eds. *Fåfängans marknad: SOM-undersökningen 2002.* Gothenburg: SOM-institutet.

Norris, P. 1999. "Introduction: The growth of critical citizens," in Norris, P. ed. *Critical Citizens. Global Support for Democratic Government.* Oxford: Oxford University Press.

Ny demokrati. 1991. *Partiprogram.* Stockholm: Ny demokrati.

Olofsson, S. 1994. "Nomineringarna delar nyd." *Svenska Dagbladet,* 21 March 1994.

Oscarsson, H. 1996. "EU-dimensionen," in Gilljam, M. and Holmberg, S. eds. *Ett knappt ja till EU.* Stockholm: Norstedts Juridik.

Oscarsson, H. 1998. *Den svenska partirymden. Väljarnas uppfattning av konfliktsstrukturen i partisystemet 1956–1996.* Gothenburg: Gothenburg Studies in Politics 54, Gothenburg University.

Pampel, F.C. 2000. *Logistic Regression: A Primer.* Thousands Oaks, CA: Sage.

Panebianco, A. 1988. *Political Parties: Organization and Power.* Cambridge: Cambridge University Press.

Pedersen, L. 1994. "Stämman blir nyd:s ödesstund." *Dagens Nyheter,* 22 May 1994.

Perrineau, P. 1997. *Le Symptôme Le Pen. Radiographie des électeurs du Front National.* Paris: Fayard.

Peruzzi, B. 1993. "Ny demokrati var ett misstag." *iDag,* 6 Februari 1993.

Peterson, T., Stigendal, M. and Fryklund, B. 1988. *Skånepartiet. Om folkligt missnöje i Malmö.* Lund: Arkiv Förlag.

Pierre, J. 1999. *Marknaden som politisk aktör—politik och finansmarknad i 1900-talets Sverige.* Demokratiutredningens forskarvolym XI, SOU 1999: 131.

Pierre, J. and Widfeldt, A. 1994. "Party organizations in Sweden: colossuses with feet of clay or flexible pillars of government?," in Katz, R.S. and Mair, P. eds. *How Parties Organize: Changes and Adaptation in Party Organizations in Western Democracies.* London: Sage.

Poggi, G. 1990. *The State. Its Nature, Development and Prospect.* Cambridge: Polity.

Putnam, R.D., Pharr, S.J. and Dalton, R.J. 2000. "Introduction: What's troubling the Trilateral democracies?," in Pharr, S.J. and Putnam, R.D. eds. *Disaffected Democracies. What's Troubling the Trilateral Countries?* Princeton: Princeton University Press.

Ribbhagen, C. 2003. "Partiernas och väljarnas dagordning vid valet 2002," in Holmberg, S. and Weibull, L. eds. *Fåfängans marknad: SOM-undersökningen 2002.* Göteborg: SOM-institutet.

Rinderheim, J. 2001. "En hederlig skattepolitik." *SD-Kuriren* 43/2001.

Rinderheim, J. 2000. "Ett nationaldemokratiskt mittenparti med ekologisk grundsyn." *SD-Kuriren* 38/2000.

Rokkan, S. 1970. *Citizens, Elections, Parties.* Oslo: Universitetsforlaget.

Ronge, P. 1993a. "Hon vägrade skriva under." *Expressen,* 20 March 1993.

Ronge, P. 1993b. "Nu är det allvar . . ." *Expressen,* 5 May 1993.

Ronge, P. 1994. "Bert jublar efter nattens drabbningar." *Expressen,* 30 March 1994.

Rose, R. and Mackie, T.T. 1988. "Do parties persist or fail? The big trade-off facing organizations," in Lawson, K. and Merkl, P.H. eds. *When Parties Fail. Emerging Alternative Organizations.* Princeton, NJ: Princeton University Press.

Rose, R. and McAllister, I. 1990. *The Loyalties of Voters. A Lifetime Learning Model.* London: Sage.

Rucht, D. 1996. "The impact of national contexts on social movement structures: a cross-movement and cross-national comparison," in McAdam, D., McCharty, J.D. and Zald, M.N. eds. *Comparative perspectives on social movements: political opportunities, mobilizing structures, and cultural framings.* Cambridge: Cambridge University Press.

Ruzza, C. 2004. "Lega Nord i Italiensk politik: vunna argument men förlorat inflytande," in Rydgren, J. and Widfeldt, A. ed. *Från Le Pen till Pim Fortuyn: Populism och parlamentarisk högerpopulism i dagens Europa.* Malmö: Liber.

Rydgren, J. 1995. *Ny demokratis uppgång och fall. En studie av det politiska manöverutrymmet.* Master Thesis. Department of Government, Uppsala University.

Rydgren, J. 1996. *Fenomenet Ny demokrati. En möjlig förklaring till partiets framväxt och framgång i riksdagsvalet 1991.* Unpublished paper. Department of Sociology, Stockholm University.

Rydgren, J. 2002. "Radical right populism in Sweden: Still a failure, but for how long?" *Scandinavian Political Studies* 26(1): 26–57.

Rydgren, J. 2003a. "Mesolevel reasons for racism and xenophobia: Some converging and diverging effects of radical right populism in France and Sweden." *European Journal of Social Theory* 6(1): 45–68.

Rydgren, J. 2003b. *The Populist Challenge: Political Protest and Ethno-nationalist Mobilization in France.* New York: Berghahn Books.

Rydgren, J. 2003c. "Varför inte i Sverige? Den radikala högerpopulismens relativa misslyckande." *Arkiv för studier i arbetarrörelsens historia* 86–87: 1–34.

Rydgren, J. 2004a. "Explaining the emergence of radical right-wing populist parties: The case of Denmark." *West European Politics* 27(3): 474–502.

Rydgren, J. 2004b. "Från skattemissnöje till etnisk nationalism: 15 år med svensk radikalhögerpopulism," in Rydgren, J. and Widfeldt, A. eds. *Från Le Pen till Pim Fortuyn: Populism och parlamentarisk högerpopulism i dagens Europa.* Malmö: Liber.

Rydgren, J. 2004c. "Mechanisms of exclusion: ethnic discrimination in the Swedish labour market." *Journal of Ethnic and Migration Studies* 30(4): 697–716.

Rydgren, J. 2004d. "The logic of xenophobia." *Rationality and Society* 16(2): 123–148.

Rydgren, J. 2005. "Is extreme right-wing populism contagious? Explaining the emergence of a new party family," *European Journal of Political Research* 44: 1–25.

Rydgren, J. and Widfeldt, A. eds. 2004. *Från Le Pen till Pim Fortuyn: Populism och parlamentarisk högerextremism i dagens Europa.* Malmö: Liber.

Sainsbury, D. 1992. "The 1991 Swedish election: protest, fragmentation, and a shift to the right." *West European Politics* 15(2): 160–166.

Sassen, S. 1996. *Losing Control? Sovereignty in an Age of Globalization.* New York: Columbia University Press.

Scarrow, S. 1996. *Parties and Their Members.* Oxford: Oxford University Press.

SCB 1994. *Statistiska meddelanden. Partisympatiundersökningen (PSU),* May 1994. Stockholm.

SCB 2000. *Statistisk årsbok för Sverige 2000.* Stockholm.

Schain, M., Zolberg, A. and Hossay, P. eds. 2002. *Shadows over Europe: The Development and Impact of the Extreme Right in Western Europe.* New York: Palgrave.

Schattschneider, E.E. 1975. *The Semisovereign People: A Realist's View of Democracy in America.* London: Wadsworth.

Schedler, A. 1996. "Anti-political-establishment parties." *Party Politics* 2(3): 291–312.

Shils, E.A. 1956. *The Torment of Secrecy. The Background and Consequences of American Security Policies.* London: Heinemann.

Sjöblom, G. 1968. *Party Strategies in a Multiparty System.* Lund: Studentlitteratur.

Skånska Dagbladet. "Fortsatt dubbelspel." 24 February 1992.

Snow, D.A. and Benford, R.D. 1992. "Master frames and cycles of protest," in Morris, A.D. and Mueller, C.M. eds. *Frontiers in Social Movement Theory*. New Haven: Yale University Press.

Snow, D.A., Rochford, Jr. E.B., Worden, S.K. and Benford, R.D. 1986. "Frame alignment processes, micromobilization, and movement participation." *American Sociological Review* 51: 464–481.

Snow, D.A., Zurcher, Jr., L.A. and Ekland-Olson, S. 1980. "Social networks and social movements: a microstructural approach to differential recruitment." *American Sociological Review* 45(5): 787–801.

Södergran, L. 1998. *Återvandringsproblematiken och svensk integrationspolitik. Senare decenniers intresse- och värderingsförskjutning*. Umeå: MERGE.

Södergran, L. 2000. *Svensk invandrar- och integrationspolitik. En fråga om jämlikhet, demokrati och mänskliga rättigheter*. Department of Sociology, Umeå University.

Sohlberg, P. and Leiulfsrud, H. 2000. "Social ojämlikhet, sociala klasser och strukturperspektiv," in Goldberg, T. ed. *Samhällsproblem*. Lund: Studentlitteratur.

Soule, S.A. 1997. "The student divestment movement in the United States and tactical diffusion: The Shantytown Protest." *Social Forces* 75(3): 855–883.

Sourander, D. 1992. "Vi låter mördare komma hit." *Göteborgsposten*, 27 July 1992.

Stenberg, E. 1994. "En profil försvinner." *Dagens Nyheter*, 7 February 1994.

Sternhell, Z. 1986. *Neither Right Nor Left. Fascist Ideology in France*. Princeton: Princeton University Press.

Stewart, A. 1969. "The social roots," in Ionescu, G. and Gellner, E. eds. *Populism. Its Meaning and National Characteristics*. London: Weidenfeld and Nicolson.

Strøm, K. 1990. "A behavioral theory of competitive political parties." *American Journal of Political Science* 34(2): 565–598.

Svallfors, S. 1989. *Vem älskar välfärdsstaten?* Lund: Arkiv.

Svallfors, S. 1997. "Välfärdsopinionen i Sverige," in *Välfärd och ojämlikhet i 20-årsperspektiv 1975–1995*. Stockholm: Statistiska centralbyrån.

Svåsand, L. and Wölund, I. 2001. "The rise and fall of the Swedish party New Democracy," Paper presented at the American Political Association's annual meeting in San Fransisco, 2001.

Svenska Dagbladet. 1992. "Ingen kan köpa Bert Karlson." 14 May 1992.

Svenska Dagbladet. 1993. "Nyd troget regeringen." 7 May 1993.

Svenska Dagbladet. 1994. "Bert Karlsson." 23 August 1994.

Sverigedemokraterna. 2002. "Partiprogram 1999 med justeringar 2002." www.sverigedemokraterna.se

Sverigedemokraterna. 2003. "Sverigedemokraternas principprogram." www.sverigedemokraterna.se

Swidler, A. 1986. "Culture in action: Symbols and strategies." *American Sociological Review* 51: 273–286.

Taggart, P. 1996. *The New Populism and New Politics. New Protest Parties in Sweden in a Comparative Perspective*. London: MacMillan Press.

Taggart, P. 2000. *Populism*. Buckingham: Open University Press.

Taguieff, P-A. 1988. *La Force du préjugé. Essai sur le racisme et ses doubles.* Paris: La Découverte.

Tarrow, S. 1998. *Power in Movement. Social Movements and Contentious Politics.* Cambridge: Cambridge University Press.

Teorell, J. 1998. *Demokrati eller fåtalsvälde. Om beslutsfattande i partiorganisationer.* Uppsala: Acta Universitatis Upsaliensis.

Ungerson, J. 1992. *Gummiankan: SAF-babyn "Ny Demokrati."* Stockholm: Aktuellt i Politiken.

Vedung, E. 1988. "The Swedish five-party syndrome and the environmentalists," in Lawson, K. and Merkl, P. eds. *When Parties Fail: Emerging Alternative Organizations.* Princeton, NJ: Princeton University Press.

Wachtmeister, I. 1988. *Ankdammen.* Stockholm: Timbro.

Wachtmeister, I. 1990. *Elefanterna.* Stockholm: Sellin & Partner Förlag.

Wachtmeister, I. 1992. *Krokodilerna.* Värnamo: AB IW Ventures.

Wachtmeister, I. and Karlsson, B. 1993. "Vi är redo att fälla regeringen." DN-debatt, Dagens Nyheter, 23 February 1993.

Weaver, R.K. and Rockman, B.A. 1993. eds. *Do Institutions Matter? Government Capabilities in the United States and Abroad.* Washington, DC: The Brookings Institute.

Weibull, L. and Holmberg, S. 1993. "Krisopinionen," in Holmberg, S. and Weibull, L. eds. *Perspektiv på krisen. SOM-undersökningen 1992.* Gothenburg: SOM-institutet.

Weibull, L. and Holmberg, S. 1994. "Vägval," in Holmberg, S. and Weibull, L. eds. *Vägval. SOM-undersökningen 1993.* Gothenburg: SOM-institutet.

Weibull, L. and Holmberg, S. 1995. "Det gamla riket," in Holmberg, S. and Weibull, L. eds. *Det gamla riket. SOM-undersökningen 1994.* Gothenburg: SOM-institutet.

Wendel, P. 1992. "Ian firade—Bert kokade," *Expressen,* 13 May 1992.

Westlind, D. 1996. *The Politics of Popular Identity. Understanding Recent Populist Movements in Sweden and the United States.* Lund: Lund University Press.

Westlind, T. 1994. "Hoppet står till Harriet." *iDag,* 24 February 1994.

Widfeldt, A. 1997. *Linking Parties with People? Party Membership in Sweden 1960–1994.* Gothenburg: Department of Political Science, Gothenburg University.

Widfeldt, A. 2000. "Scandinavia: mixed success for the populist Right." *Parliamentary Affairs* 53(3): 468–500.

Widfeldt, A. 2004. "The diversified approach: Sweden," in Eatwell, R. and Mudde, C. eds. *Western Democracies and the New Extreme Right Challenge.* London: Routledge.

Wieviorka, M. 1998. *Le racisme, une introduction.* Paris: La Découverte.

Windeskog, J. 1999. "Politik är *inte* att vilja." *SD-Kuriren* 35/1999.

Worsley, P. 1969. "The concept of populism," in Ionescu, G. and Gellner, E. eds. *Populism. Its Meaning and National Characteristics.* London: Weidenfeld and Nicolson.

Zald, M.N. and Ash, R. 1966. "Social movement organizations: growth, decay and change." *Social Forces* 44(3): 327–341.

INDEX